P9-ARJ-646

The Basic Training of Pavlo Hummel

A PLAY

By David W. Rabe

WITHDRAWN

SAMUEL FRENCH, INC.

25 WEST 45TH STREET   NEW YORK 10036

7623 SUNSET BOULEVARD   HOLLYWOOD 90046

LONDON   *TORONTO*

LITTLE COUNTRY THEATER

Dept. of Speech & Drama

North Dakota State Univ.

FARGO, NORTH DAKOTA 58102

Copyright ©, 1969, by David W. Rabe

ALL RIGHTS RESERVED

*CAUTION: Professionals and amateurs are hereby warned that THE BASIC
TRAINING OF PAVLO HUMMEL is subject to a royalty. It is fully protected under
the copyright laws of the United States of America, the British Commonwealth,
including Canada, and all other countries of the Copyright Union. All rights,
including professional, amateur, motion pictures, recitation, lecturing, public
reading, radio broadcasting, television, and the rights of translation into foreign
languages are strictly reserved. In its present form the play is dedicated to the
reading public only.*

*THE BASIC TRAINING OF PAVLO HUMMEL may be given stage presentation
by amateurs upon payment of a royalty of Fifty Dollars for the first performance,
and Twenty-five Dollars for each additional performance, payable one week before
the date when the play is given, to Samuel French, Inc., at 25 West 45th Street, New
York, N. Y. 10036, or at 7623 Sunset Boulevard, Hollywood, Calif. 90046, or to
Samuel French (Canada), Ltd., 80 Richmond Street East, Toronto, Ontario,
Canada M5C 1P1.*

*Royalty of the required amount must be paid whether the play is presented for
charity or gain and whether or not admission is charged.*

Stock royalty quoted on application to Samuel French, Inc.

*For all other rights than those stipulated above, apply to Ellen Neuwald, 905
West End Ave., New York, N. Y. 10025.*

*Particular emphasis is laid on the question of amateur or professional readings,
permission and terms for which must be secured in writing from Samuel French,
Inc.*

*Copying from this book in whole or in part is strictly forbidden by law, and the
right of performance is not transferable.*

*Whenever the play is produced the following notice must appear on all programs,
printing and advertising for the play: "Produced by special arrangement with
Samuel French, Inc."*

*Due authorship credit must be given on all programs, printing and advertising
for the play.*

**Anyone presenting the play shall not commit or authorize
any act or omission by which the copyright of the play or the
right to copyright same may be impaired.**

**No changes shall be made in the play for the purpose of your
production unless authorized in writing.**

Printed in U.S.A.

ISBN 0 573 60587 4

CAST

PAVLO
YEN
ARDELL
SGT. TOWER
CAPTAIN (*all officers*)
KRESS
PARKER
PIERCE
CORPORAL
GRENNEL
HINKLE
BURNS
HENDRIX
RYAN
MICKEY
MRS. SORRENTINO
MRS. HUMMEL
JONES
MAMASAN
BRISBEY
SGT. WALL
PARHAM
VARIOUS SOLDIERS
VARIOUS VIETNAMESE

TIME AND PLACE

The United States Army—1965–1967

The Basic Training
of Pavlo Hummel

ACT ONE

*The set is a space, a platform slanting upward from the
downstage area. The floor is nothing more than slats
that seem to run in various directions with a military precision. It has a brownish color. The backdrop is dark, touches of green. Along the back of the
set runs a ramp that is elevated about two feet off
the floor. Stage L. and a little down from the ramp
stands the drill sergeant's tower. This element is
stark and as realistic as is possible. Further downstage and stage L. the floor opens into a pit two feet
deep. There is an old furnace partly visible. Downstage and stage R. are three army cots with foot-
lockers at their base. Upstage and stage R. there is
the bar area: an army ammunition crate and an army
oil drum set as a table and chair before a fragment
of the metal wall that is covered partly with beer
can labels. All elements of the set should have some
military tone to them, some echo of basic training.
To start the play, pop American music is heard for
an instant in the dark. Then LIGHTS UP on the
bar area: evening. A drunken G.I. sits slumped on
the crate and leaning forward on the drum.* YEN
(*pronounced "Ing"*), *a Vietnamese girl dressed in
purple silk pajamas, slacks and pull-over top, moves
about with a beer, trying to settle* PAVLO *down.*

PAVLO. (*Dressed in fatigues, moving with the music,
dealing somehow with everyone in the room as he
speaks.*) Did I do it to him? The triple-Hummel. Can
you hear your boy? (*A sort of shudder runs through his
shoulders: he punches.*) A little shuffle and then a triple

5

boom-boom-boom. Ain't I bad, man. Gonna eat up Cleveland. Gonna piss on Chicago. (*Banging with his palms on the sides of the oil drum.*)

YEN. Creezy, creezy.

PAVLO. Dinky dow!

SOLDIER. (*Disturbed by the banging, looking up, deeply drunk.*) Les . . . go . . . home. . . .

YEN. Pavlo creezy.

PAVLO. Dinky dow.

YEN. Pavlo boucoup love. Sleep me all time. . . .

PAVLO. Did I ever tell you?—Thirteen months a my life ago— Joanna was her name. Serrafino, a little bit a guinea-wop made outa all the pins and sticks all bitches are made a. And now I'm the guy who's been with the Aussies. I HAD TEA WITH 'EM. IT WAS ME THEY CALLED TO— Hummel! MEDIC! (*With a fairly good Australian accent.*) "The dirty little blighters blew me bloody arm off." (*And* YEN *brings a beer.*) Yeh, girl, in a little bit a time. (*And back to the air.*) We had a cat, you know? So we had a kitty box, which is a place for the cat to shit.

YEN. Talk "shit." I can talk "shit." Numba ten talk.

PAVLO. Ohhh, damn that Serrafino, what she couldn't be taught. And that's what I'd like to do—look her up and explain a few things like, "Your face, Serrafino, I don't like your ugly face." Did I ever tell you about the ole lady? Did I ever speak her name, me mudda?

YEN. Mudda you, huh, Pavlo? Very nice.

PAVLO. To be seen by her now, oh, she would shit her jeans to see me now, up tight with this little odd-lookin' whore, feelin' good, and tall, ready to bed down. Ohhh, Jesus Mahoney. You see what she did, she wrote Joanna a letter. My mother. She called Joanna a dirty little slut and when I found out I cried, I wailed, baby, big tears, I screamed and threw kitty litter; I threw it in the air, I screamed over and over, "Happy Birthday, Happy Birthday," and then one day there was Joanna in the subway and she said "Hello" and told me my favorite jacket I was wearing made me look ugly, didn't fit, made me look fat. (*The grenade hits with a lond clump in the room, having been thrown by a hand that merely flashed between the curtains and everyone looks without moving.*) GREEENADE!

(*And by now* PAVLO *has moved. He has the grenade in his hand, and there comes the explosion, loud, extremely loud, and the LIGHTS go black, go red, or blue, the girl screams, the bodies fly. And a soldier,* ARDELL, *a black man in a uniform that is strangely unreal, perhaps gray in color, or perhaps khaki, but with black ribbons and medals. He wears sunglasses, bloused boots. He appears distantly, far* U., *at the* C. *A body detail is moving in the side at the instant he speaks, two men carrying a stretcher. They wear fatigues, helmets.*)

ARDELL. You want me, Pavlo? You callin'? Don't I hear you? Yeh, yeh, that the way it happen sometimes. Everybody hit, everybody hurtin', but the radio ain't been touched, the dog didn't feel a thing; the engine's good as new but all the people dead and the chassis a wreck, man. (*The* STRETCHERMEN *have come in to remove the body of the dead G.I. The body of the girl and of* MAMASAN *have vanished in the explosion. The radio has continued to play until the point where* ARDELL, *speaking, has turned it off.*) Yeh, yeh, some mean motherfucker, you don't even see, blow you away. Don't I hear you callin'? (*Pivoting, moving swiftly down* C.) Get off it. Bounce on up here. (*And* PAVLO *leaps to his feet, runs to join* ARDELL.)

PAVLO. Pfc Pavlo Hummel, sir, RA-74-313-226.

ARDELL. We gonna get you your shit straight. No need to call me "sir."

PAVLO. I know . . . you. I saw you die.

ARDELL. That right. Now what's your unit? Now shout it out.

PAVLO. Second of the Sixteenth; First Division. BIG
RED ONE. . . .

ARDELL. Company.

PAVLO. Echo.

ARDELL. C.O.?

PAVLO. My Company Commander is Captain M. W.
Henderson. My Battalion Commander is Lt. Colonel Roy
J. S. Tully.

ARDELL. Platoon?

PAVLO. Third.

ARDELL. Squad.

PAVLO. Third.

ARDELL. Squad and platoon leaders.

PAVLO. My platoon leader is 1st Lt. David R. Barnes;
my squad leader is Staff Sergeant Peter T. Collins.

ARDELL. You got family?

PAVLO. No.

ARDELL. You lyin', boy.

PAVLO. One mother; one half brother.

ARDELL. All right.

PAVLO. Yes.

ARDELL. Soldier, what you think a the war?

PAVLO. It's being fought.

ARDELL. Ain't no doubt about that.

PAVLO. No.

ARDELL. You kill anybody?

PAVLO. Yes.

ARDELL. Like it?

PAVLO. Yes.

ARDELL. Have nightmares?

PAVLO. Pardon?

ARDELL. What we talkin' about, boy?

PAVLO. No.

ARDELL. How tall you, you lyin' motherfucker?

PAVLO. Five-ten.

ARDELL. Eyes.

PAVLO. Green.

ARDELL. Hair.

PAVLO. Red.

ARDELL. Weight.

PAVLO. 152.

ARDELL. What you get hit with?

PAVLO. Hand grenade. Fragmentation-type.

ARDELL. Where about it get you?

PAVLO. (*Touching himself.*) Here. And here. Mostly in the abdominal and groin areas.

ARDELL. Who you talkin' to? Don't you talk that shit to me, man. Abdominal and groin areas, that shit. It hit you in the stomach, man, like a ten-ton truck and it hit you in the balls, blew 'em away. Am I lyin'?

PAVLO. (*Able to grin, glad to grin.*) No, man.

ARDELL. Hurt you bad?

PAVLO. Killed me.

ARDELL. That right. Made you dead. You dead, man; how you feel about that?

PAVLO. Well . . .

ARDELL. DON'T YOU KNOW? I THINK YOU KNOW! I think it piss you off. I think you lyin' you say it don't. Make you wanna scream.

PAVLO. Yes.

ARDELL. You had that thing in your hand, didn't you? What was you thinkin' on, you had that thing in your hand?

PAVLO. About throwin' it. About a man I saw when I was eight years old who came through the neighborhood with a softball team called the DEMONS and he could do anything with a softball underhand that most big leaguers can do with a hardball overhand. He was fantastic.

ARDELL. That all?

PAVLO. Yes.

ARDELL. You ain't lyin'?

PAVLO. No. (*A WHISTLE and* FIGURES *move behind* PAVLO *and* ARDELL, *a large* GROUP OF MEN *in fatigues without markings other than their name tags and U.S. Army. There are a good number of them. And on a*

*high Drill Instructor's tower, dimly lit at the moment,
is a large* NEGRO SERGEANT. *A* CAPTAIN *observes from the
distance. A* CORPORAL *prowls among them, checking
buttons, etc.*) Who're they?

ARDELL. Man, don't you jive me. You know who they
are. That Fort Gordon, man. They Echo Company, 8th
Battalion, Third Training Regiment. They basic training,
baby.

PAVLO. (*Removing Pfc stripes and 1st Division patch.*)
Am I . . . really . . . dead . . . ?

ARDELL. Damn near, man; real soon. Comin' on. Eight
more weeks. Got wings as big as streets. Got large, large
wings.

PAVLO. I saw you die, now you're watchin' me . . .
Ardell . . . ?

ARDELL. Whatever you say, Pavlo.

PAVLO. Sure. You saw me. That grenade come rollin'
out. You scooped it under you. I—

ARDELL. New York, huh? Where'bouts?

PAVLO. Manhattan. 231 East 45th.

ARDELL. Okay. Now we know who we talkin' about.
Somebody say "Pavlo Hummel," we know who they
mean.

SGT. TOWER. GEN'L'MEN! (*As the men snap to
Parade Rest and* PAVLO, *startled, runs to find his place
among them.*) You all lookin' up here and can you see
me? Can you see me well? Can you hear and comprehend
my words? Can you see what is written here? Over my
right tit-tee, can you read it? Tower. My name. And I
am bigger than my name. And can you see what is sewn
here upon the muscle of my arm? Can you see it? AN-
SWER!

MEN. No. (*The* MEN *all stand in ranks below the
tower.*)

SGT. TOWER. No, what? WHAT?

MEN. NO, SERGEANT.

SGT. TOWER. It is also my name. It is my first name.
SERGEANT. That who I am. I you Field First. And

you gonna see a lot a me. You gonna see so much a me, let me tell you, you gonna think I you mother, father, sisters, brothers, aunts, uncles, nephews, nieces, and children—if-you-got-'em—all rolled into one big black man. Yeh, gen'l'men. And you gonna become me. You gonna learn to stand tall and be proud and you gonna run as far and shoot as good. Or else you gonna be ashamed; I am one old man and you can't outdo no thirty-eight-year-old man, you ashamed. AM I GONNA MAKE YOU ASHAMED? WHAT DO YOU SAY?

MEN. Yes, Sergeant!

SGT. TOWER. NO! NO, GEN'L'MEN. No, I am not gonna make you ashamed. SERGEANT, YOU ARE NOT GONNA MAKE US ASHAMED.

MEN. SERGEANT, YOU ARE NOT GONNA MAKE US ASHAMED.

SGT. TOWER. WE ARE GONNA DO EVERYTHING YOU CAN DO AND DO YOU ONE BETTER!

MEN. WE ARE GONNA DO EVERYTHING YOU CAN DO AND DO YOU ONE BETTER!

SGT. TOWER. YOU A BUNCH A LIARS. YOU A BUNCH A FOOLS! Now you listen up; you listen to me. No one does me one better. And especially no people like you. Don't you know what you are? TRAINEES! And there ain't nothin' lower on this earth except for one thing and we all know *what* that is, do we not, gen'l'men?

MEN. *Yes*, Sergeant!

SGT. TOWER. And what is that? (*Pause.*) You told me you knew! Did you lie to me? Oh, no, nooo, I can't believe that; please, please, don't lie. Gen'l'men, did you lie?

MEN. Yes, Sergeant.

SGT. TOWER. No, no, please. If there something you don't know, you tell me. If I ask you something, you do not know the answer, let me know. Civilians. That the answer to my question. The only creatures in this world lower than trainees is civilians, and we hate them all. All. (*Quick pause.*) And now . . . and finally . . . and most important, do you see what is written here? Over my heart; over my left tit-tee, do you see? U.S. ARMY. Which is where I live. Which is where we all live. Can you, gen'l'men, can you tell me you first name now, do you know it? (*Quick pause.*) Don't you know? I think you do, yes, I do, but you just too shy to say it. Like little girls watchin' that thing just get bigger and bigger for the first time, you shy. And what did I tell you to do when you don't know the answer I have asked?

MEN. What is our first name?

SGT. TOWER. You! . . . You there! (*Suddenly pointing into the ranks.*) You! Ugly! Yeah, you. That right. You ugly. Ain't you? You TAKE ONE BIG STEP FORWARD. (*And it is* PAVLO *stepping forward.*) I think I saw you were not in harmony with the rest of these men. I think I saw that you were looking about at the air like some kinda fool and that malingering, trainee, and that intol'able. So you drop, you hear me? You drop down on you ugly little hands and knees and lift up you butt and knees from off that beautiful Georgia clay and you give me TEN and that's push-ups of which I am speaking. (PAVLO *begins the push-ups:* TOWER *goes back to the* MEN.) NOW YOU ARE TRAINEES, ALL YOU PEOPLE, AND YOU LISTEN UP. I ask you WHAT IS YOUR FIRST NAMES, YOU TELL ME "TRAINEE"!

MEN. TRAINEE!

SGT. TOWER. TRAINEE, SERGEANT!

MEN. TRAINEE, SERGE—

SGT. TOWER. I CAN'T HEAR YOU!

MEN. *TRAINEE, SERGEANT!*

SGT. TOWER. AND WHAT IS YOUR LAST NAMES? YOUR OWN LAST FUCKING NAMES? (*The* MEN *shout a chorus of American names.*) AND YOU LIVE IN THE ARMY OF THE UNITED STATES OF AMERICA.

MEN. AND WE LIVE IN THE ARMY OF THE UNITED STATES OF AMERICA.

SGT. TOWER. WITH BALLS BETWEEN YOUR

LEGS! YOU HAVE BALLS! NO SLITS! BUT BALLS, AND YOU— (*Having risen,* PAVLO *is getting back into ranks.*)

MEN. AND WE HAVE BALLS BETWEEN OUR LEGS! NO SLITS, BUT BALLS!

SGT. TOWER. (*Suddenly back to* PAVLO.) Ugly! Now who told you to stand? Who you think you are, you standin', nobody tole you to stand. You drop. You drop, you hear me? (*And* PAVLO *goes back into the push-up position.*) What your name, boy?

PAVLO. Yes, sir.

SGT. TOWER. Your name, boy!

PAVLO. Trainee Hummel, sir!

SGT. TOWER. Sergeant.

PAVLO. Yes, sir.

SGT. TOWER. Sergeant. I AM A SERGEANT!

PAVLO. SERGEANT! YOU ARE A SERGEANT!

SGT. TOWER. All right. That nice; all right, only in the future, you doin' push-ups, I want you countin' and that countin' so loud it scare me so I think there some kinda terrible, terrible man comin' to get me, am I understood?

PAVLO. Yes, Sergeant.

SGT. TOWER. I can't hear you!

PAVLO. Yes, Sergeant! Yes, Sergeant!

SGT. TOWER. All right! You get up and fall back where you was. Gen'l'men. You are gonna fall out. By platoon. Which is how you gonna be doin' 'most everything from now on—by platoon and by the numbers—includin' takin' a shit. Somebody say to you, ONE, you down; TWO, you doin' it; THREE, you wipin' and you ain't finished, you cuttin' it off. I CAN'T HEAR YOU!

MEN. YES, SERGEANT.

SGT. TOWER. I say to you SQUAT, and you all hunkered down and got nothin' to say to anybody but HOW MUCH? and WHAT COLOR, SERGEANT?

MEN. Yes, Sergeant.

SGT. TOWER. You good people. You a good group. Now I gonna call you to attention and you gonna snap-to,

that's heels on a line or as near it as the conformation
of your body permit; head up, chin in, knees not locked;
you relaxed. Am I understood?

MEN. Yes—

SGT. TOWER. AM I UNDERSTOOD, GODDAMNIT,
OR DO YOU WANT TO ALL DROP FOR TWENTY
OR—

MEN. YES, SERGEANT, YES, SERGEANT!

ARDELL. PAVLO, MY MAN, YOU ON YOUR WAY.

CORPORAL. PLATOOOON! PLATOOOON!

SGT. TOWER. I GONNA DO SOME SINGIN', GEN'-
L'MEN, I WANT IT COMIN' BACK TO ME LIKE
WE IN GRAND CANYON—

CORPORAL. TEN-HUT!

ARDELL. DO IT, GET IT!

SQUAD LEADERS. RIGHT FACE!

SGT. TOWER. —AND YOU MY MOTHERFUCKIN'
ECHO!

CORPORAL. FORWARD HARCH!

SGT. TOWER. LIFT YOUR HEAD AND LIFT IT
HIGH!

MEN. —LIFT YOUR HEAD AND LIFT IT
HIGH—

SGT. TOWER. ECHO COMPANY PASSIN' BY!

MEN. ECHO COMPANY PASSIN' BY!

ARDELL. (*And the* MEN *are going off in groups during
this.*) MOTHER, MOTHER, WHAT'D I DO?

MEN. MOTHER, MOTHER, WHAT'D I DO?

ARDELL. THIS ARMY TREATIN' ME WORSE
THAN YOU!

MEN. THIS ARMY TREATIN' ME WORSE THAN
YOU!

SGT. TOWER. LORD HAVE MERCY I'M SO BLUE!

MEN. LORD HAVE MERCY I'M SO BLUE! IT
EIGHT MORE WEEKS TILL WE BE THROUGH!
IT EIGHT MORE WEEKS TILL WE BE THROUGH!
IT EIGHT MORE WEEKS TILL WE BE THROUGH!

(*And all the* MEN *have marched off in lines of four or five in different directions, giving a sense of large numbers, a larger space and now, out of this movement, comes a spin off of two men,* KRESS *and* PARKER *coming down the* C. *of the stage, yelling the last lines of the song, marching, stomping, then breaking and running* L. *and into the furnace room. There is the hulk of the belly of the furnace, the flickering of the fire.* KRESS *is large, muscular, with a constant manner of small confusion as if he feels always that something is going on that he nearly, but not quite, understands. Yet there is something seemingly friendly about him.* PARKER *is smaller: he wears glasses.*)

KRESS. I can't stand it, Parker, bein' so cold all the time and they're all insane, Parker. Waxin' and buffin' the floor at 5:30 in the morning is insane. And then you can't eat till you go down the monkey bars and you gotta eat in ten minutes and can't talk to nobody, and no place in Georgia is warm. I'm from Jersey. I can jump up in the air, if there's a good wind. I'll land in Fort Dix. Am I right so far? So Sam gets me. What's he do? Fort Dix? Uh-uh. Fort Gordon, Georgia. So I can be warm, right? Down South, man. Daffodils and daisies. Year round. (*Hollering.*) BUT AM I WARM? DO YOU THINK I'M WARM? DO I LOOK LIKE I'M WARM? JESUS H! EVEN IN THE GODDAMN FURNACE ROOM, I'M FREEZIN' TA DEATH!

PARKER. So, what the hell is hollerin' like a stupid ape gonna do except to let 'em know where we at?

KRESS. (*As* PAVLO *enters* U., *moving slowly in awe toward the tower, looking.*) Heat up my blood!

ARDELL. (*To* PAVLO.) What you doin' strollin' about like a fool, man, you gonna have people comin' down all over you, don't you know—

OFFICER. (*Having just entered.*) What're you doin' walkin' in this company area? Don't you know you run in this company area? Hummel, you drop, you hear me, you drop.

(PAVLO *goes into push-up position and starts to do the ten push-ups.*)

ARDELL. (*Over him.*) Do 'em right, do 'em right!

KRESS. Why can't I be warm? I wanna be warm.

PARKER. Okay, man, you're warm.

KRESS. No; I'm not; I'm cold, Parker. Where's our goddamn fireman, don't he ever do nothin' but push-ups? Don't he ever do nothin' but trouble!

PARKER. Don't knock that ole boy, Kress, I'm tellin' you; Hummel's gonna keep us laughin'!

KRESS. Yesterday I was laughin' so hard. I mean, I'm stupid, Parker, but Hummel's *stupid*. I mean, he volunteers to be fireman 'cause he thinks it means you ride in a raincoat on a big red truck and when there's nothin' to do you play cards.

PARKER. Yeah! He don't know it means you gotta baby-sit the goddamn furnace all night, every night. And end up lookin' like a stupid chimney sweep!

KRESS. Lookin' what?

PARKER. (*As PIERCE enters at a jog, moving across the stage toward ARDELL and PAVLO, the officer having exited after the order.*) Like a goddamn chimney sweep!

PAVLO. Where you goin'?

PIERCE. (*Without hesitating.*) Weapons room and furnace room.

PAVLO. (*Getting to his feet.*) Can I come along?

PIERCE. (*Still running, without looking back.*) I don't give a shit. (*Exits, PAVLO following as ARDELL is drifting in the opposite direction.*)

PAVLO. . . . great . . .

KRESS. Yeh? Yeh, Parker, that's good. Chimney sweeps!

PARKER. Yeh, they were these weird little men always crawlin' around, and they used to do this weird shit ta chimneys.

(PIERCE *and* PAVLO *enter. They have their rifles.* PIERCE *is a trainee acting as a squad leader. He has a cloth marked with corporal stripes on his left sleeve.*)

PIERCE. At ease!

KRESS. Hey, the Chimney Shit. Hey, what's happenin', Chimney Shit?

PAVLO. How you doin', Kress?

KRESS. Where's your red hat, man?

PAVLO. What?

PARKER. Ain't you got no red fireman's hat?

PAVLO. I'm just with Pierce, that's all. He's my squad leader and I'm with him.

PARKER. Mr. Squad Leader.

PAVLO. Isn't that right, Pierce?

PARKER. Whose ass you kiss to get that job, anyway, Pierce?

PIERCE. At ease, trainees.

KRESS. He's R.A., man. Regular Army. Him and Hummel. Lifer morons. Whata they gonna do to us today, anyway, Mr. Actin' Sergeant Corporal? What's the lesson for the day: first aid or bayonet? I love this fuckin' army.

PIERCE. The schedule's posted, Kress!

KRESS. You know I don't read, man; hurts my eyes; makes 'em water.

PAVLO. When's the gas chamber, that's what I wanna know?

KRESS. For you, Chimney Shit, in about ten seconds when I fart in your face.

PAVLO. I'm all right. I do all right.

KRESS. Sure you do, except you got your head up your ass.

PAVLO. Yeh? Well, maybe I'd rather have it up my ass than where you got it. (*Slight pause: it has made no sense to* KRESS *at all.*)

KRESS. What?

PAVLO. You heard me, Kress.

KRESS. What'd he say, Parker? (*There is frenzy in*

this.) I heard him, but I don't know what he said. WHAT'D YOU SAY TO ME, HUMMEL?

PAVLO. Just never you mind, Kress.

KRESS. I DON'T KNOW WHAT YOU SAID TO ME, YOU WEIRD PERSON!

PARKER. (*Patting* KRESS.) Easy, man, easy; be cool.

KRESS. But I don't like weird people, Parker. I don't like them. How come I gotta be around him? I don't wanna be around you, Hummel!

PAVLO. Don't you worry about it, I'm just here with Pierce. I just wanna know about the gas chamber.

KRESS. It's got gas in it! Ain't that right, Parker! It's like this goddamn giant asshole, it farts on you. THHPP-BBBZZZZZZZZ! (*Silence*.)

PAVLO. When is it, Pierce?

KRESS. Ohhhhh, Jesus, I'm cold.

PAVLO. This ain't cold, Kress.

KRESS. I know if I'm cold.

PAVLO. I been colder than this. This ain't cold. I been a lot colder than—

KRESS. DON'T TELL ME IT AIN'T COLD OR I'LL KILL YOU! JESUS GOD ALMIGHTY, I HATE THIS MOTHER ARMY STICKIN' ME IN WITH WEIRD PEOPLE! DIE, HUMMEL! Will you please do me that favor! Oh, God, let me close my eyes and when I open them, Hummel is dead. Please, please. (*Squeezes his eyes shut, clenches his hands for about two seconds and then looks at* PAVLO *who is grinning*.)

PAVLO. Boy, I sure do dread that gas chamber.

KRESS. He hates me, Parker, he truly hates me.

PAVLO. No, I don't.

KRESS. What'd I ever do to him, you suppose?

PARKER. I don't know, Kress.

PAVLO. I don't hate you.

PARKER. How come he's so worried about that gas chamber, that's what I wonder.

PAVLO. Well, see, I had an uncle die in San Quentin. (KRESS *screams*.) That's the truth, Kress. (KRESS

screams again.) I don't care if you believe it. He killed
four people in a fight in a bar.

PARKER. Usin' his bare hands, right?

PAVLO. You know how many people are executed
every damn day in San Quentin? One hell of a lot. And
every one of 'em just about is somebody's uncle and one
of 'em was my uncle Roy. He killed four people in a
bar room brawl usin' broken bottles and table legs and
screamin', jus' screamin'. He was mean, man. He was
rotten; and my folks been scared the same thing might
happen to me; all their lives, they been scared. I got
that same look in my eyes like him.

PARKER. What kinda look is that?

KRESS. That really rotten look, man. He got that
really rotten look. Can't you see it?

PAVLO. You ever steal a car, Kress? You know how
many cars I stole?

KRESS. Shut up, Hummel! You're a goddamn chimney
sweep and I don't wanna talk to you because you don't
talk American, you talk Hummel! Some goddamn foreign
language!

PARKER. How many cars you stole?

PAVLO. Twenty-three.

KRESS. Twenty-three!

(PARKER *whistles.*)

PAVLO. That's a lotta cars, huh?

PARKER. You damn betcha, man. How long'd it take
you, for chrissake? Ten years?

PAVLO. Two.

PARKER. Workin' off and on, you mean.

PAVLO. Sure. Not every night, or they'd catch you.
And not always from the same part of town. Man, sometimes I'd hit lower Manhattan, and then the next night
the Bronx or Queens and sometimes I'd even cut right on
outa town. One time, in fact, I went all the way to New
Haven. Boy, that was some night because they almost
caught me. Can you imagine that? Huh? Parker? Huh?

Pierce? All the way to New Haven and cops on my tail
every inch a the way, roadblocks closin' up behind me,
bang, bang, and then some highway patrolman, just as I
was wheelin' into New Haven, he come roarin' outa this
side road. See, they must a called ahead or somethin' and
he come hot on my ass. I kicked it, man, arrrrgggggghh-
hhh . . . ! 82 per. Had a Porsche; he didn't know who
he was after; that stupid fuzz, 82 per, straight down the
gut, people jumpin' outa my way, kids and businessmen
and little old ladies, all of 'em, and me kickin' ass, up to
97 now, roarin' baby sirens all around me so I cut into
this alley and jump. Oh, Jesus, Christ, just lettin' the
car go, I hit, roll, I'm up and runnin' down for this
board fence, up and over, sirens all over now, I mean,
all over, but I'm walkin' calm, I'm cool. Cops are goin'
this way and that way. One of 'em asks me if I seen
a Porsche go by real fast. Did *I* see—

KRESS. *Jesus-goddamn*—the furnace room's smellin'
like the gas chamber! (*Rising to leave*, PARKER *following*.)

PARKER. Right, Hummel. That's right. I mean, I liked
your story about your really rotten uncle Roy better than
the one about all the cars.

KRESS. Les go get our weapons, will ya?

PARKER. Defend our fuckin' selves.

PAVLO. I'll see . . . you guys later. (*Half calling, half
to himself as they are gone. Silence.*) Hey, Pierce, you
wanna hear my General Orders; make sure I know 'em,
O.K.? Like we're on Guard Mount and you're the O.D.
. . . You wanna see if I'm sharp enough to be one a
your boys. O.K.? (*Snapping to attention.*) Sir! My first
general order is to take charge of this post and all government property in view, keeping always on the alert
and . . .

PIERCE. Gimme your eighth, Hummel.

PAVLO. Eighth? No, no, lemme do 'em 1, 2, 3. You'll
mess me up.

PIERCE. That's the way it's gonna be, Hummel. The

man comes up to you on Guard Mount he's gonna be all over you—right on top a you yellin' down your throat. You understand me? He won't be standin' back polite and pretty lettin' you run your mouth.

PAVLO. Just to practice, Pierce. I just wanna practice.

PIERCE. You don't wanna practice shit. You just wanna stand there and have me pat your goddamned head for bein' a good boy. Don't you know we stood here laughin' at you lyin' outa your ass? Don't you have any pride, man?

PAVLO. I got pride. And anyway, they didn't know I was lyin'.

PIERCE. Shit.

PAVLO. And anyway, I wasn't lyin', it was story telling. They was just messin' with me a little, pickin' on me. My mom used to always tell my dad not to be so hard on me, but he knew.

(WHISTLE blows loudly from off.)

PIERCE. Let's go.

PAVLO. See, he was hard on me, 'cause he loved me. I'm R.A., Pierce.

PIERCE. You got a R.A. prefix, man, but you ain't Regular Army.

PAVLO. They was just jumpin' on me a little; pickin' on me.

(Again the WHISTLE.)

PIERCE. That whistle means formation, man.

PAVLO. They're just gonna draw weapons; I already got mine.

PIERCE. That ain't what I said, Jerkoff!

PAVLO. Well, I ain't goin' out there to stand around doin' nothin' when I can stay right here and put the time to good use practicin' D & D. *(Again the WHISTLE. The* MEN *are gathering, we hear their murmuring.)*

PIERCE. You ain't no motherin exception to that whistle, Hummel!

PAVLO. You ain't any real corporal anyway, Pierce. So don't get so big with me just because you got that hunk a thing wrapped around you—

PIERCE. Don't you mess up my squad, Hummel! Don't you make me look bad or I'll get you your legs broken.

PAVLO. (*As the whistle blows and* PIERCE *is leaving and gone.*) I bet you never heard a individual initiative.

(*WHISTLE again as* SOLDIERS *rush in to line up in formation at Parade Rest while* SGT. TOWER *climbs to stand atop the platform.*)

ARDELL. They don't know, do they? They don't know who they talkin' to.

PAVLO. No.

ARDELL. You gonna be so straight.

PAVLO. So clean. (SGT. TOWER *notices that someone is missing from formation. He turns, descends, exits.*) Port Harms! (*And he does it with only a slight and quickly corrected error.*)

ARDELL. Good, Pavlo. Good. (*Slight pause.*) Order Harms!

PAVLO. (*Does it. There is some skill in the move.*) Okay. . . .

ARDELL. RIGHT SHOULDER . . . HARMS . . . !

(*And* PAVLO *does this, but there is the head flinch, the rifle nicking the top of his helmet. His back is toward the* GROUP *and* SGT. TOWER *enters, watches for a time.*)

PAVLO. Goddamnit. Shit. (*Again the rifle back to order.*)

ARDELL. RIGHT SHOULDER . . .

PAVLO. HARMS! (*Again it is not good.*) You mother rifle. You stupid fucking rifle. RIGHT SHOULDER, HARMS. (*He tries.*) Mother! Stupid mother, whatsamatter with you? I'll kill you! (*And he has it high above his head. He is looking up.*) Rifle, please. Work for me, do it for me. I know what to do, just you do it.

ARDELL. Just go easy. Man . . . just easy. It don't mean that much. What's it matter?

SGT. TOWER. What you doin', trainee?

PAVLO. (*Snapping to attention.*) Yes, sir! Trainee Pavlo Hummel, sir.

SGT. TOWER. I didn't ask you you name, boy. I asked you what you doin' in here when you supposed to be out on that formation?

PAVLO. Yes, sir.

SGT. TOWER. No, I don't have no bars on my collar, do you see any bars on my collar?

PAVLO. No . . . no . . .

SGT. TOWER. But what do you see on my sleeve at about the height a my shoulder less a little, what do you see?

PAVLO. Stripes, Sergeant. Sergeant stripes.

SGT. TOWER. So how come you call me sir? I ain't no sir. I don't want to be no sir. I am a sergeant. Now do we know one another?

PAVLO. Yes, Sergeant.

SGT. TOWER. That mean you can answer my question in the proper manner, do it not?

PAVLO. I was practicin' D & D, Sergeant, to make me a good soldier.

SGT. TOWER. Ohhhhhhh! I think you tryin' to jive this ole man, that what you doin'. Or else you awful stupid because all the good soldiers is out there in that formation like they supposed to when they hear that whistle. Now which?

PAVLO. Pardon, Sergeant?

SGT. TOWER. Which is it? You jivin' on me or you awful stupid, you take your pick. And lemme tell you why you can't put no jive on the old Sarge. Because long time ago, this ole Sarge was one brand-new, baby-soft, smart-assed recruit. So I see you and I say "What that young recruit doin' in that furnace room this whole company out there bein' talked at by the CO? And the answer come to me like a blast a thunder and this voice sayin' to me in my head, "This here young recruit jerkin' off, that what he doin'," and then into my head come this picture and we ain't in no furnace room, we in that jungle catchin' hell from this one little yellow man and his automatic weapon that he chained to up on top of this hill. "Get on up that hill!" I tell my young recruit. And he tell me, "Yes, Sergeant," like he been taught, and then he start thinkin' to hisself, "What that ole Sarge talkin' about, 'run on up that hill,' Ah git my ass blown clean away. I think maybe he got hit on his head, he don't know what he's talkin' about no more—maybe I go on over behind that ole rock—practice me a little. D & D." Ain't that some shit the way them young recruits wanna carry on? So what I think we do, you and me, long about 2200 hours we do a little D & D and PT and all them kinda alphabetical things. Make you a good soldier.

PAVLO. I don't think I can, Sergeant. That's night time, Sergeant, and I'm a fireman. I got to watch the furnace.

SGT. TOWER. That don't make me no never mind. We jus' work it in between your shifts. You see? Ain't it a wonder how you let the old Sarge do the worryin' and figurin' and he find a way? (*Turning, starting to leave.*)

PAVLO. Sergeant, I was wondering how many push-ups you can do. How many you can do that's how many I want to be able to do before I ever leave.

SGT. TOWER. Boy, don't you go sayin' no shit like that, you won't ever get out. You be an ole bearded blind fuckin' man pushin' up all over Georgia.

PAVLO. (*And* PAVLO, *speaking immediately and rapidly, a single rush of breath, again stops* SGT. TOWER. *Incredulously* SGT. TOWER *watches, starts to leave, watches.*) And I was wondering also, Sergeant Tower, and wanted to ask you—when I was leaving home, my mother wanted to come along to the train station, but I lied to her about the time. She would have wanted to hug me right in front of everybody. She would have waved a handkerchief at the train. It would have been awful. (*And* SGT. TOWER *now leaves, is gone.* PAVLO *calls.*) She would have stood there, waving. Was I wrong?

CORPORAL. TEN HUT! FORWARD HARCH!

(*And the* MEN *begin to march in place. And* PAVLO, *without joining them, also marches.*)

SGT. TOWER. AIN'T NO USE IN GOIN' HOME.

MEN. (*Beginning to exit.*) AIN'T NO USE IN GOIN' HOME.

SGT. TOWER. (*At the side of the stage.*) JODY GOT YOUR GAL AND GONE.

MEN. JODY HUMPIN' ON AND ON.

SGT. TOWER. AIN'T NO USE IN GOIN' BACK. (*And* PAVLO, *in his own area, is marching away.*)

MEN. JODY GOT OUR CADILLAC.

CORPORAL. AIN'T NO MATTER WHAT WE DO.

ALL. JODY DOIN' OUR SISTER TOO.

CORPORAL. Count cadence, delayed cadence, count cadence count!

ALL. 1—2—3—4. 1, 2, 3, 4. 1234. *Hey!*

(ALL *are gone now except* PAVLO, *who comes spinning out of his marching pattern to come stomping to a halt in the furnace room area while* ARDELL. *drifts toward him.*)

ARDELL. Oh, yeh; army train you, shape you up—teach you all kinds of good stuff. Like Bayonet. It all about what you do you got no more bullets and this man after you. So you put this knife on the end a your rifle, start yellin' and carryin' on. Then there hand to hand. Hand to hand, cool. It— (PAVLO *is watching, listening.*) all about hittin' and kickin'. What you do when you got no gun and no knife. Then there C.B.R. CBR:

Chemical, Biological and Radiological Warfare. What you do when some mean motherfucker hit you with some kinda chemical. You (ARDELL *mimes throwing a grenade at* PAVLO.) got green fuckin' killin' smoke all around you. What you gonna do? You gotta git on your protective mask. You ain't got it?

PAVLO. (*Choking.*) But I'm too beautiful to die. (*Rummaging about in the furnace room until* ARDELL *throws him a mask.*)

ARDELL. But you the only one who believe that, Pavlo. You gotta be hollerin' loud as you know how, "GAS." And then, sweet lord almighty, little bit later, you walkin' along, somebody else hit you with some kinda biological jive. But you know your shit. Mask on.

PAVLO. GAS! GAS! GAS!

ARDELL. You gettin' it, Pavlo. All right. Lookin' real good. But now you tired and you still walkin' and you come up on somebody bad—this boy mean—he hit you with radiation. (PAVLO *goes into a tense, defensive posture.*)

PAVLO. Awww. (*Realizing his helplessness.*)

ARDELL. That right. You know what you do? You kinda stand there, that what you do, whimperin' and talkin' to yourself, 'cause he got you. You gotta be some kinda fool, somebody hit you with radiation, man, you put on a mask, start hollerin', "Gas." Am I lyin'? Pavlo. What do you say?

PAVLO. Aww, no. . . . No, man— No, no.— (*And there has been, toward the end of this, a gathering of a group of* SOLDIERS *in T shirts and underwear, T shirts and trousers in the barracks area.* PAVLO, *muttering in denial of the radiation, crosses the stage hurriedly, fleeing the radiation, running into* PARKER *who grabs him, spins him.*) I did not.

KRESS. The hell you didn't!

PARKER. You been found out, Jerk-off. (*Kneeling behind* PAVLO *to take a billfold from his pocket.*)

PAVLO. No.

KRESS. We got people saw you. Straight, honest guys.

PARKER. Get that thing off your face. (*Meaning the mask.*)

BURNS. The shit I didn't see you.

PARKER. You never saw a billfold before in your life, is that what you're tryin' to say? You didn't even know what it was?

KRESS. Is that what you're tryin' to say, Hummel?

PAVLO. No.

KRESS. What are you tryin' to say?

PAVLO. I'm goin' to bed. (*Moving toward his bed but stopped by* KRESS.)

KRESS. We already had two guys lose money to some thief around here, Shitbird, and we got people sayin' they saw you with Hinkle's billfold in your pudgy little paws.

HINKLE. (*Deep Southern drawl.*) Is that right, Hummel? (*As* PARKER *hands him the billfold he found on* PAVLO.)

PAVLO. I was just testin' you, Hinkle, to see how stupid you were leavin' your billfold layin' out like that when somebody's been stealin' right in our own platoon. What kinda army is this anyway? You're supposed to trust people with your life, you can't even trust 'em not to steal your money.

PARKER. Listen to him.

PAVLO. That's the truth, Parker. I was just makin' a little test experiment to see how long it'd be before he'd notice it was gone. I don't steal.

KRESS. What about all them cars?

PAVLO. What cars?

PARKER. The New Haven Caper, Jerk-off. You know.

PAVLO. Ohhh, that was different, you guys. That was altogether different.

KRESS. Yeh, they were cars and you couldn't fit them in your pocket.

PAVLO. Those people weren't my friends.

PARKER. You don't steal from your friends. That what

you're sayin'? Kress, Hummel says he don't steal from his friends.

KRESS. (*Jumping up on* PAVLO's *bed, standing, walking about.*) Don't that make his prospects pretty damn near unlimited?

PAVLO. Hey! Kress; what're you doin'?

KRESS. What?

PAVLO. I said, "What're you up to?" You're on my bed.

KRESS. Who is?

PAVLO. You are. You are.

KRESS. Where?

PAVLO. Right here. You're on my bed. That's my bed.

KRESS. No, it isn't. It's not anybody's. It's not yours, Hummel.

PAVLO. It is too.

KRESS. Did you buy it?

PAVLO. Get off my bed, Kress!

KRESS. If you didn't buy it, then how is it yours, Ugly!

PAVLO. It was given to me.

KRESS. By who?

PAVLO. You know by who, Kress. The army gave it to me. Get off it.

KRESS. Are you going to take it with you when you leave here? If it's yours, you ought to be planning on taking it with you; are you?

PAVLO. I can't do that.

KRESS. You're taking people's billfolds; you're taking their money; why can't you take this bed?

PAVLO. Because it was just loaned to me.

KRESS. Do you have any kind of papers to prove that? Do you have papers to prove that this is your bed?

PAVLO. There's proof in the orderly room; in the orderly room, or maybe the supply room and you know it. That bed's got a number on it somewhere and that number is like its name and that name is by my name on some papers somewhere in the supply room or the orderly room.

KRESS. Go get them.

PAVLO. What do you mean?

KRESS. Go get them. Bring them here.

PAVLO. I can't.

KRESS. If they're yours, you can.

PAVLO. They're not my papers, it's my bed. Get off my bed, Kress. (KRESS *now kneels down, taking a more total possession of the bed.*) Goddamnit, Kress. GOD-DAMNIT! (*Silence:* KRESS *has not moved, seems in fact about to lie down.*) All right. Okay. You sleep in my bed, I'm gonna sleep in yours.

(EVERYONE *stands around watching as* PAVLO *charges off stage toward where* KRESS' *bed is located.*)

KRESS. (*Rising up a little, tense, looking off, as all look off in the direction* PAVLO *has gone.*) No, Hummel. (*Warning in* KRESS' *voice.*)

PAVLO. The hell I ain't, Kress.

KRESS. No, no, I strongly advise against it. I do strongly so advise. Or something awful might happen. I might get up in the middle of the night to take a leak and stagger back to my old bed. Lord knows what I might think you are . . . laying there. Lord knows what I might do.

PAVLO. (*Yelling from off.*) Then get out of my bed.

KRESS. You don't understand at all, do you, shitbird! I'm sleeping here. This is where I'm going to sleep. You not going to sleep anywhere. You're going to sit up, or sleep on the floor, whatever. And in the morning, you're going to make this bed. This one. Because if you don't it'll be unmade when Sgt. Tower comes to inspect in the morning and as we've already discussed, there's papers somewhere in one room or another and they show whose bed this is.

PAVLO. (*Rushing back, stomping, raging.*) GOD-

DAMN YOU, KRESS, GET OUT OF MY BED! GET
OFF MY BED! GET OUT OF IT!

(*WHISTLE blows and* EVERYONE *scrambles to firing
range. There is the popping of many rifles firing as
on the back platform at the very rear of the set,
three or four of the* MEN *are in firing positions,
others stand behind them at Port Arms until* SGT.
TOWER *calls "CEASE FIRE" and the firing stops.
The* MEN *who have been firing put their rifles on
their shoulders to be cleared.* SGT. TOWER *walks behind them tapping each on the head when he has
seen the weapon is clear. The* MEN *leap to their feet.*
SGT TOWER *then steps out in front of them, begins
to pace up and down.*)

SGT. TOWER. GEN'L'MEN! IT GETTIN' TOWARD
DARK NOW AND WE GOT TO GET HOME. IT A
LONG LONG WAYS TO HOME AND OUR MOTH-
ER'S GOT SUPPER READY WAITING FOR US.
WHAT CAN WE DO? WE GOT TO GET HOME
FAST AS WE CAN, WHAT CAN WE DO? DO ANY-
BODY HAVE AN IDEA? LET ME HEAR YOU
SPEAK IF YOU DO? I HAVE AN IDEA. ANYBODY
KNOW MY IDEA? LET ME HEAR YOU IF YOU
DO.
    PAVLO. Run . . .
    BURNS. Run?
    SGT. TOWER. WHAT?
    MORE MEN. RUN!
    SGT. TOWER. I CAN'T HEAR YOU.
    MEN. WHAT?
    SGT. TOWER. RUN!
    MEN. RUN!
    SGT. TOWER AND THE MEN. RUN! RUN! RUN!
RUN! RUN!
    SGT. TOWER. PORT HARMS—WHOOO! DOUBLE
TIME! WHOOO!

(*They have been running in place. Now* SGT. TOWER
*leads them off. They exit, running, reappear, exit
again. Reappear, spreading out now, though* PAVLO
is fairly close behind SGT. TOWER, *who enters once
again and runs to a point downstage where he turns
to* PAVLO *entering, staggering, leading.*)

SGT. TOWER. FALL OUT! (*And* PAVLO *collapses, the
others struggle in, fall down.*)

PIERCE. FIVE GODDAMN MILES! (*All are in ex-
treme pain.*)

KRESS. MOTHER-GODDAMN-BITCH—I NEVER
RAN NO FIVE GODDAMN MILES IN MY LIFE.
YOU GOTTA BE CRAZY TO RUN FIVE GODDAMN
MILES. . . .

PARKER. I hurt. I hurt all over. I hurt, Kress. Oh,
Christ.

PIERCE. There are guys spread from here to Range 2.
You can be proud you made it, Parker. The whole company, man; they're gonna be comin' in for the next ten
days.

(*And* PARKER *yells in pain.*)

KRESS. Pierce, what's wrong with Parker?

PARKER. SHIT TOO, YOU MOTHER!

KRESS. It'll pass, Parker. Don't worry. Just stay easy.
(*And a little separate from the* OTHERS, PAVLO *is about
to begin doing push-ups. He is very tired. It hurts him to
do what he's doing.*) Oh, Hummel, no. Hummel, please.
(*He is doing the push-ups, breathing the count softly.*)
Hummel, you're crazy. You really are. He really is,
Parker. Look at him. I hate crazy people. I hate 'em.
YOU ARE REALLY CRAZY, HUMMEL. STOP IT
OR I'LL KILL YOU. (PAVLO, *saying the number of
push-ups, stopping, pivoting into a sit-up position.*) I
mean, I wanna know how much money this platoon lost
to that thief we got among us.

PIERCE. Three hundred and twelve dollars.

KRESS. What're you gonna do with all that money?

PAVLO. Spend it. Spend it.

KRESS. Something gonna be done to you! You hear me, weird face? You know what's wrong with you? You wouldn't know cunt if your nose was in it. You never had a piece a ass in your life.

(*And there is a loud blast on a WHISTLE.*)

PAVLO. Joanna Sorrentino ga'me so much ass my mother called her a slut.

KRESS. YOU FUCKING IDIOT!

(*Again the WHISTLE.*)

PIERCE. Oh, Christ . . .

PAVLO. Let's go. LET'S GO. LET'S GET IT.

KRESS. Shut up.

PAVLO. Let's GO, GO, GO— (*Moving—ALL exit.*)

KRESS. SHUT YOUR MOUTH, ASSHOLE!

PAVLO. LET'S—GO, GO, GO, GO, GO, GO, GO. . . . (*Yelling, leading, yelling.*)

(*As a LIGHT goes on on the opposite side of the stage and there are TWO SOLDIERS there with pool cues at a pool table. There are no pool balls. The game will be pantomime. One of them is the CORPORAL. They use a cue ball to shoot and work with.*)

HENDRIX. You break.

CORPORAL. Naw, man, I shoot break on your say so, when I whip your ass, you'll come cryin'. You call. (*Flipping a coin as PAVLO comes running back to get his helmet left where he was doing the pushups.*)

HENDRIX. Heads.

CORPORAL. You got it.

(*As PAVLO, scurrying off with his helmet, meets SGT. TOWER entering from opposite side.*)

SGT. TOWER. Trainee, go clean the Day Room. Sweep it up.

PAVLO. Pardon, Sergeant? I forgot my helmet. . . .

SGT. TOWER. Go clean the Day Room, trainee.

(*As at the pool game,* HENDRIX *shoots break.*)

CORPORAL. My . . . my . . . my . . . Yes, sir. You're gonna be tough all right. That was a pretty damn break all right. (*Moving now to position himself for his shot.*) Except you missed all the holes. Didn't nobody tell you you were supposed to knock the little balls in the little holes?

PAVLO. (*Entering.*) Sergeant Tower said for me to sweep up the Day Room.

SECOND SOLDIER. And that's what you do—you don't smile, laugh or talk, you sweep.

CORPORAL. You know what buck a ball means, trainee?

PAVLO. What?

CORPORAL. Trainee's rich, Hendrix. Can't go to town, got money up the ass.

PAVLO. Sure I know what "buck a ball" means.

CORPORAL. Ohh, you hustlin' trainee motherfucker. New game. Right now. Rack 'em up!

(HENDRIX *moves as if to re-rack the balls.*)

PAVLO. You sayin' I can play?

CORPORAL. Hendrix, you keep an eye out for anybody who might not agree trainee can relax a bit. You break, man.

PAVLO. I'll break.

CORPORAL. That's right.

PAVLO. You been to the war, huh? That's a 1st Division Patch you got there, ain't it? (*Shooting first shot, missing, not too good.*)

CORPORAL. That's right.

PAVLO. Where at?

CORPORAL. How many wars we got?

PAVLO. I mean exactly where.

CORPORAL. (*Lining up his shot.*) Di An. Ever hear of it?

PAVLO. Sure.

CORPORAL. Not much of a place but real close to Da Nang. (*He shoots, watches, moves for the next shot.*)

PAVLO. You up there too?

CORPORAL. Where's that?

PAVLO. By Da Nang. (CORPORAL *is startled by* PAVLO *knowing this. He shoots and misses here. He stands now facing* PAVLO.) I mean, I thought Di An was more down by Saigon. Down there. They call that D. Zone, don't they?

CORPORAL. You're right, man, you know your shit. We got us a map-readin' motherfucker, Hendrix. Yeh, I was by Saigon, Hummel.

PAVLO. I thought so.

CORPORAL. Your shot. (*Has moved off to the side and* HENDRIX *who has a hip flask of whiskey.*)

PAVLO. (*Moving for his shot.*) Big Red One, man, I'd be proud wearin' that. (*And he shoots.*) Shit. (*Having missed.*)

CORPORAL. (*Moving again to the table.*) Good outfit. Top kinda outfit. Mean bastards. Everyplace we went, man, we used ta tear 'em a new asshole. You can believe me. (*Shooting, making it, he moves on.*) I'm gonna win all your damn money, man. You got orders yet for where you go when you're finished with basic?

PAVLO. No.

CORPORAL. Maybe if you're lucky, you'll get infantry, huh? Yeh, yeh. I seen some shit, you can believe me. (*And during the following long speech, he moves about the table, shooting, shooting, running the table, as he speaks.*) But you go over there, that's what you're goin' for. To mess with them people, because they don't know nothin'. Them slopes; man, they're the stupidest bunch a people anybody ever saw. It don't matter what you do

to 'em or what you say, man, they just look at you.
They're some kinda goddamn phenomenon, man. Can of
bug spray buy you all the ass you can handle in some
places. Insect repellant, man. You ready for that? You
give 'em can a bug spray, you can lay their 14-year-old
daughter. Not that any of 'em screw worth a shit. (*Slight
pause.*) You hear a lot a people talkin' Airborne, 173d,
101st Marines, but you gotta go some to beat the First
Division. I had a squad leader, Sergeant Tinden. He'd
been there two goddamn years when I got there, so he
knew the road, man; he knew his way. So we was comin'
into this village once, the whole company and it was supposed to be secure. We was Charlie Company and Alpha'd
been through already, left a guard. And we was lead
platoon and lead squad and comin' toward us on the path
is this old man, he musta been a hundred, about three
foot tall and he's got this little girl by the hand and she's
maybe a half-step behind him. He's wavin' at us, "OK,
OK, G.I." And she's wavin', too, but she ain't sayin'
nothin', but there's this funny noise you can hear, a kind
of cryin' like. (*He still moves about, shooting, speaking,
pausing, judging which shot to take.*) Anyway, I'm next
to the Sarge and he tells this ole boy to stop, but they
keep comin' like they don't understand, smilin' and
wavin', so the Sarge says for 'em to stop in Vietnamese
and then I can see that the kid is cryin'; she's got big
tears runnin' outa her eyes, and her eyes are gettin'
bigger and bigger and I can see she's tuggin' at the old
man's hand to run away but he holds her and he hollers
at her and I'm thinkin', "Damn, ain't that a bitch, she's
so scared of us." And Tinden, right then, man, he
dropped to his knees and let go two bursts—first the old
man, then the kid, cuttin' them both right across the face,
man, you could see the bullets walkin'. It was somethin'.
(*In silence he sets and takes his last shot. He flops the
cue onto the table.*) You owe me, man; thirteen bucks.
But I'm superstitious, so we'll make it twelve. (*As* PAVLO
is paying.) That's right. My ole daddy—the last day he

saw me—he tole me good—"Don't you ever run on nobody, Boy, or if you do I hope there's somebody there
got sense enough to shoot you down. Or if I hear you got
away, I'll kill you myself." There's folks like that runnin'
loose, Hummel. My o'e man. You dig it. (*And* PAVLO *is
staring at him.*) What the fuck are you lookin' at?

PAVLO. I don't know why he shot . . . them.

CORPORAL. Satchel charges, man. The both of them,
front and back. They had enough T.N.T. on 'em to blow
up this whole damn state and the kid got scared. They
was wearing it under their clothes.

PAVLO. And he knew . . .

CORPORAL. That's right. Been around; so he knew.
You ready, Hendrix? (*They are moving to exit.*)

HENDRIX. Ain't that some shit, Hummel? Ain't that the
way to be?

PARKER. (*Far across the stage. In dimness. Crouching,
peering toward where* PAVLO *is. Nearby,* KRESS *is with
three or four other* SOLDIERS, *crouching among the beds.*)
Dear Mother. It was the oddest thing last night. I sat
near my bunk, half awake, half asleep. . . .

CORPORAL. You keep your ear to the ground, Hummel,
you're gonna be all (*Exiting.*) right. We'll see you around.

PAVLO. Just to see and to move; just to move. (*Mim-
ing with his broom or just his hands, the firing of a rifle
while* ARDELL *stares at him across the table and lunges
suddenly backwards, rapidly hauling the table off.*)

PARKER. Yes, yes, good mother, I could not sleep, I
don't know why. And then for further reasons that I do
not know, I happened to look behind me and there . . .
was a space ship, yes, a space ship, green and golden,
good mother, come down to the sand of our Georgia
home. A space ship. (*He is referring to* KRESS *and the*
OTHERS *as they hide. He speaks loudly, flamboyantly.*
KRESS *kneels downstage with a blanket.* PAVLO *wanders
nearer, nearer.*) And out of it, leaping they came, little
green men no larger than pins. "Good Lord in Heaven,"
said I to myself. "What do they want? Sneaking among

us, ever in silence, ever in stealth." Then I saw Hummel.
Hummel is coming, said I. I will ask Hummel, said I to
myself. Hummel is coming. (KRESS *and the* OTHERS *are
stationed as if near a door through which* PARKER *is
looking and toward which* PAVLO *is now moving as if to
enter the barracks.*) THIEF!

(*Blanket is thrown over him. He is dragged to the floor.
They beat and kick him, calling him "thief." He
cries out. Squirms. A se ond blanket is thrown upon
him, a mattress. It is his own bedding they are
using, and as they beat and kick him, a WHISTLE
blows, all but* PAVLO *go running out, grabbing rifles
and helmets as they go to form up for bayonet practice.* SGT. TOWER *is there.*)

PAVLO. (*Emerging from beneath the blankets—no one
is there.*) Didn't I do enough push-ups? How many do
you have to do, Ardell?

ARDELL. You got to understand, Pavlo, it fun sometimes to get a man the way they got you. Come down on
him, maybe pivot kick. Break his fuckin' spine. Do him,
man. Do . . . him . . . good.

SGT. TOWER. (*Standing atop his platform, bayonet in
hand.*) You got to know this bayonet shit, gen'l'men, else
you get re-cycled, you be back to learn it all again. Eight
more beautiful weeks in the armpit a the nation. Else you
don't get recycled, you get killed. Then you wish for
maybe half a second, you been recycled. Do you know
the spirit of the bayonet is to kill? What is the spirit of
the bayonet?

MEN. To kill! (*While* PAVLO *stirs about and* PIERCE
enters the barracks area.)

SGT. TOWER. You sound like pussies. You sound like
slits.

MEN. TO KILL! (PAVLO *is still on the floor, does not
see* PIERCE.)

SGT. TOWER. You sound like pussies. (PIERCE *is disheveled, a little drunk.*)

MEN. TO KILL! (*Freeze.*)

PIERCE. (*To* PAVLO, *who grabs inside his footlocker for a book.*) Look at you. Ohhh, you know how much beer I hada drink to get fucked up on 3.2 beer? Hummel, look at me. You think it's neat to be squad leader? It's not neat to be squad leader. (PAVLO *has been pretending to read from the little book he has gotten from his locker.*) I hear you got beat up this afternoon.

PAVLO. I got a blanket party.

PIERCE. You're in my squad and other guys in my squad beat you, man; I feel like I oughta do somethin'. I'm older, see? Been to college a little; got a wife. And I'm here to tell you, even with all I seen, sometimes you are unbelievable, Hummel.

PAVLO. I don't care. I don't care.

PIERCE. I mean, I worry about you and the shit you do, man.

PAVLO. You do what you want, Pierce.

PIERCE. I mean, that's why people are after you, Hummel. That's why they fuck with you.

PAVLO. I'm trying to study my code a conduct, Pierce, you mind? It's just not too damn long to the proficiency test. Maybe you oughta be studyin' your code a conduct too, insteada sneakin' off to drink at the P.X.

PIERCE. I wanna know how you got those rocks down your rifle. It's a two mile walk out to the rifle range, and you got rocks in your barrel when we get there. That's what I'm talkin' about.

PAVLO. I don't know how that happened.

PIERCE. And every fight you get into, you do nothin' but dance, man. Round in a circle, bobbin' and weavin' and gettin' smacked in the mouth. Man, you oughta at least try and hit somebody. JESUS CHRIST, Hummel, what's wrong with you? We're in the shower and I tell you to maybe throw a punch once in a while, step with it, pivot, so you try it right there on that wet floor and damn near kill yourself smashin' into a wall.

PAVLO. Fuck you, Pierce.

PIERCE. Fuck you, Hummel. (*Silence.*)

PAVLO. You know somethin', Pierce? My name ain't even really Pavlo Hummel. It's Michael Hummel. I had it legally changed. I had my name changed.

PIERCE. You're puttin' me on.

PAVLO. No, no, and someday, see, my father's gonna say to me, "Michael, I'm so sorry I ran out on you," and I'm gonna say, "I'm not Michael, Asshole. I'm not Michael anymore." Pierce? You weren't with those guys who beat up on me, were you?

ARDELL. Sometimes I look at you, I don't know what I think I'm seein', but it sooo simple. You black on the inside. In there where you live, you that awful hurtin' black so you can't see yourself no way. Not up or down or in or out. (*And* PAVLO *begins making his bunk and Bayonet begins.*)

SGT. TOWER. (*Having descended from the platform; moves among the* MEN.) There ain't no army in the world got a shorter bayonet than this one we got. Maneuverability. It the only virtue. You got to get inside that big long knife that other man got. What is the spirit of the bayonet?

MEN. TO KILL!

SGT. TOWER. You sound like pussies.

MEN. TO KILL!

SGT. TOWER. You sound like slits!

MEN. TO KILL!

SGT. TOWER. EN GARDE!

MEN. AGGGH!

SGT. TOWER. LONG THRUST, PARRY LEFT . . . WHOOOOOO!

MEN. AGGGH!

(*And the* MEN *make the move, one of them stumbling, falling down, clumsy, embarrassed.*)

SGT. TOWER. Where you think you are? You think you in the movies? This here real life, gen'l'men. You actin' like there ain't never been a war in this world. Don't you know what I'm sayin'? You got to want to put this steel into a man. You got to want to cut him, hurt him, make him die. You got to want to feel the skin and muscle come apart with the push you give. It come to you in the wood. RECOVER AND HOLD!

MEN. AGGGH! (*And the* MEN *make the move, they yell and growl with each thrust. Another falls down, gets up.*)

SGT. TOWER. EN GARDE!

MEN. AGGGH!

SGT. TOWER. Lookin' good, lookin' good. Only you ain't mean. (MEN *growl.*) How come you ain't mean? (MEN *growl again.*) HORIZONTAL BUTT STROKE SERIES, WHOOO! (*And they make the move, much more complicated this time. There is the thrust, recovery, then uppercutting butt stroke, horizontal butt stroke and finally the downward slash. The growling and yelling is louder this time.*) Look at you; look at you. Ohhh, but you men put into my mind one German I saw in the war, I got one bullet left, don't think I want to shoot it, and here come this goddamned big-assed German. "Agggg-hhhh," I yell to him and it a challenge and he accept. "Agggghhhh," he say to me and set hisself and I just shoot him. Boom! Ohhh, he got a look on his face like I never saw before in my life. He one baffled motherfucker, Jim. (*Without command, the* MEN *begin to march.*)

ARDELL.

ONCE A WEEK I GET TO TOWN . . .

MEN.

THEY SEE ME COMIN' THEY ALL LAY DOWN.

ARDELL.

IF I HAD A LOWER I.Q. . . .

(ALL *are marching now, exiting.*)

MEN.

I COULD BE A SERGEANT TOO.

SGT. TOWER.
LORD HAVE MERCY, I'M SO BLUE.
MEN.
LORD HAVE MERCY, I'M SO BLUE.
SGT. TOWER.
IT SIX MORE WEEKS TILL I BE
THROUGH.
MEN.
IT SIX MORE WEEKS TILL WE BE
THROUGH.
SGT. TOWER.
SOUND OFF!
MEN.
1—2—

(BURNS, PIERCE, FIRST SOLDIER *enter barracks area, still
singing as others are still exiting, and these three
men set up the crap game on a footlocker.*)

SGT. TOWER.
SOUND OFF.
(OTHERS *enter*, PAVLO, HINKLE.)
MEN.
3—4. CADENCE COUNT. 1—2—3—4. 1—2.
3-4.

(*The counting ends.* MEN *are spread around the barracks.*)

PAVLO. (*Talking to* HINKLE. *A crap game goes on
nearby.*) Can you imagine that, Hinkle? Just knowin'.
Seein' nothin' but bein' sure enough to gun down two
people. They had T.N.T. on 'em; they was stupid slope-
heads. That Sergeant Tinden saved everybody's life. I
get made anything but infantry, I'm gonna fight it, man.
I'm gonna fight it. You wanna go infantry with me,
Hinkle. You're infantry and good at it, you're your own
man. I'm gonna wear my uniform everywhere when I'm

home, Hinkle. My mother's gonna be so excited when she sees me. She's just gonna yell. I get nervous when I think about if she should hug me. You gonna hug your mother when you get home?

HINKLE. My mom's a little bitty skinny woman.

PAVLO. I don't know if I should or shouldn't.

HINKLE. What's your mom like?

PIERCE. You tellin' him about your barn house exploits, Hinkle?

HINKLE. Oh, no.

PIERCE. Hinkle says he screwed sheep. He tellin' you that, Hummel?

PARKER. How about pigs, Hinkle?

HINKLE. Oh, yeh.

KRESS. I'm tellin' you, Parker, it was too much; all that writin' and shit, and runnin' around. They ain't got no right to test you. Proficiency test, proficiency test; I don't even know what a proficiency is—goddamn people —crawlin' and writin'—I'm tellin' you they ain't got no right to test you. They get you here, they mess with you—they let you go. Who says they gotta test you?

PIERCE. (*Who has the dice and is laying down money.*) Who's back man? I'm shootin' five.

KRESS. I got so nervous in hand-to-hand, I threw a guy against the wall. They flunked me for bein' too rough.

PIERCE. Who's back man?

KRESS. I'll take three. (*Putting down money.* PARKER *drops a couple of ones.*) I get re-cycled, I'll kill myself, I swear it. (*As* PIERCE *is shaking the dice, saying over and over, "Karen loves me, Karen loves me."*) I'll cut off my ear.

PIERCE. (*Throwing the dice.*) Karen says I'm GOOD!

KRESS. Goddamn! Shit! How they do it again, Parker?

PARKER. Pierce, you're incredible.

KRESS. Parker!

PARKER. They add up your scores, man; your P.T. plus your rifle, plus the score they got today. Then they divide by 3. You lettin' it ride, Pierce? (*Throwing down a five.*)

PIERCE. Karen loves me.

KRESS. Where they get the "3"? (*Putting in money.*)

PARKER. There's three events, man.

PIERCE. (*Throwing the dice.*) Karen say, "I know the road!"

KRESS. You fucking asshole!

PARKER. Goddamnit, Pierce!

PIERCE. Who wants me? Back man's got no heart. Shootin' twenty I come 7 or 11—double or nothin'. Whose twenty says I can't come for all out of the gate . . .

(*A SOLDIER enters on the run.*)

GRENNEL. Tower's right behind me; he's got the scores.

(*General commotion as SGT. TOWER strides across the stage and enters their area.*)

PIERCE. TENHUT! (*All come to attention before their bunks.*)

SGT. TOWER. AT EASE! (MEN *to Parade Rest.*) Gen'-men. It's truth and consequences time. The sad tidings and the (*Handing a paper to PIERCE for him to post it on the board.*) glad tidings. You got two men in this platoon didn't make it. They Burn and Kress. They gonna have to stay here eight more weeks and if they as dumb as it look, maybe eight more after that and eight fuckin' more. The rest a you people, maybe you ain't got no spectacular qualities been endowed upon my mind, but you goin' home when you figured. (*Turning and leaving.*)

PIERCE. TENHUT!

SGT. TOWER. (*Exiting.*) Carry on.

(*They are silent a moment: KRESS stands.*)

PIERCE. Lemme holler . . . just one . . . time, lemme holler . . .

HINKLE. Mother, mother, make my bed!

A SOLDIER. (*At the bulletin board.*) Me! My name! Me!

PIERCE. AGGGGGGGHHHHHHHHHHHHHHHHHHH-AAAA!

PARKER. Lemme just pack my bags!

HENDRIX. (*Entering with civilian clothes, shirt, trousers, on a hanger, hat on his head.*) Lookee— lookee—

HINKLE. What're them funny clothes?

PIERCE. CIVILIAN CLOTHES! CIVILIAN—

HINKLE. CI-WHOL-IAN?

PIERCE. PEOPLE OUTSIDE, MAN! THAT'S WHY THEY AIN'T ALL FUNNY AND GREEN, BECAUSE YOU'RE OUTSIDE WHEN YOU WEAR 'EM. YOU'RE BACK ON THE BLOCK. BACK IN THE WORLD!

PAVLO. DON'T NOBODY HEAR ME CALLIN' "KRESS!" (*He has said the name a few times during the yelling. He is atop his own bed.*) I think we oughta tell him how sorry we are he didn't make it. I'm gonna. I'm gonna tell him. I'm sorry, Kress, that you're gonna be re-cycled and you're not goin' home. I think we're all sorry. I bet it's kinda like gettin' your head caught in a blanket, the way you feel. It's a bad feelin', I bet, and I think I understand it even if I am goin' back where there's lights and it's pretty. I feel sorry for you, Kress, I just wanna laugh, I feel so sorry— (*And* KRESS *pushes him off the bed, leaping after him.* PAVLO *staggers ba`k- ward.*) Sonofabitch, what're you— SONOFABITCH! (*Swinging a wild right hand, they flail and crash about,* KRESS *grabbing* PAVLO'S *wrist, drawing him forward, snapping the arm up into a hammer lock.*)

KRESS. Down. Don't you hear me? Down, I'm sayin'. Don't you hear me? Thata boy. . . . Called crawlin'. . . . (*And* PAVLO *has been thrown to the floor,* KRESS *diving on top of him.*) You got the hang of it . . . now.

. . . Crawlin'. . . . Yeh. Now I'm gonna ask you something? Okay?

PAVLO. Okay . . .

KRESS. What I'd like to know is who is it in this platoon steals money from his buddies? Who is it don't know how to talk decent to nobody? and don't have one goddamn friend? Who is that person? You tell me, Hummel? The name a that person passed his test today by cheatin' (*Twisting the arm.*)

PAVLO. I don't . . . know. . . . (*The whole of this is furious; both men are wild.*)

KRESS. Who? (*Working the arm.*)

PAVLO. No— (*And the arm is twisted again.*) Stop him, somebody. Pierce. You're my squad leader, Pierce. Ohhhh . . . Pierce, please. . . . Aggghhhh . . . Pierce . . .

KRESS. WHO? (*And PAVLO yells.*)

PIERCE. Ease off a little . . .

KRESS. I CAN'T HEAR YOU!

PIERCE. Kress, I—

PAVLO. HUMMEL!

KRESS. WHAT? WHAT?

PAVLO. HUMMEL! HUMMEL!

KRESS. WHAT?

PAVLO. HUMMEL! HUMMEL! He did 'em. All of those things. All of 'em. He cheated. He cheated. HUMMEL! HUM—

PIERCE. Kress, goddamnit. GODDAMNIT! (*Pulling him away. Leaping to lift KRESS away from PAVLO and throw him sideways.*)

KRESS. (*Leaving PAVLO, pulling free of PIERCE.*) What? What you want, Corporal? Don't mess with me, man. (*Staring at PIERCE who is now between him and PAVLO. KRESS backs away; yet he is raging.*) Don't mess with Kress. Not when he's feelin' bad. He'll kill ya, honest to God. He'll pee in your dead mouth. (*And PAVLO rushes at KRESS, howling.*)

PIERCE. Nooooooooo. (*Seizing PAVLO.*)

PAVLO. I'm all right. I'm all right. I do all right!

PIERCE. Will you listen to me, man; you're goin' home, not Kress. You got him.

PAVLO. Fucking asshole!

PIERCE. Will you listen? (*Shoving* PAVLO *back toward* c. *Scolding him, blocking his pursuit of* KRESS, *backing him up.*) You gotta learn to think, Hummel. You gotta start puttin' 2 and 2 together so they fit. You beat him; you had ole Kress beat and then you fixed it so you hadda lose. You went after him so he hadda be able to put you down.

PAVLO. I just wanted to let him know what I thought.

PIERCE. No, no!

PAVLO. He had no call to hit me like that. I was just talkin'—

PIERCE. You dared him, man.

PAVLO. You shoulda stopped him, that's the problem. You're the squad leader. That's just this whole damn army messin' with me and it ain't ever gonna end but in shit. How come you're a squad leader? Who the fuck are you? I'm not gonna get a chance at what I want. Not ever. Nothin' but shit. They're gonna mess with me— make a clerk outa me or a medic or truck driver, a goddamn moron—or a medic—a nurse—a fuckin' Wac with no tits—or a clerk, some little goddamn twerp of a guy with glasses and no guts at all. So don't gimme shit about what I done, Pierce, it's what you done and done and didn't— (*And during this whole thing,* PIERCE, *squad leader, has moved about straightening the bunks, foot-lockers disturbed by the fight and* PAVLO, *in growing desperation, has followed him. Now* PIERCE, *in disgust, starts to leave.*) That's right; keep on walkin' away from your duties, keep—

PIERCE. You're happy as a pig in shit, I don't know why I keep thinkin' you ain't.

PAVLO. I am not.

PIERCE. Up to your eyeballs!

PAVLO. I'm gonna kill myself, Pierce! (*It bursts out of him.*)

PIERCE. If you weren't in my squad, I'd spit in your face. . . .

PAVLO. Fuck you, fuck you. (*Rocking backward, bowing then forward.*) I hate you goddamn people.

ARDELL. I know. (*And* PAVLO'S *bending carries him down to the floor.*)

PAVLO. Ardell. (*At his footlocker,* PAVLO *rummages about.*)

ARDELL. I know. I know. All you life like a river and there's no water all around—this emptiness—you gotta fill it. Gotta get water. You dive, man, you dive off a stone wall (PAVLO *sits, canteen and paper bag in his hands.*) into the Hudson River waitin' down dark under you, for a second, it's all air . . . so free . . . do you know the distance you got to fall? You think you goin' up. Don't nobody fall up, man. Nobody.

PAVLO. What is it? I want to know what it is. The thing that Sergeant saw to make him know to shoot that kid and old man. I want to have it, know it, be it.

ARDELL. I know.

PAVLO. When?

ARDELL. Soon.

PAVLO. If I could be bone, Ardell; if I could be bone. In my deepest part or center, if I could be bone. (*Taking a container from the bag, he takes pills, washes them down with water, while* SGT. TOWER, *already on the platform, speaks and* PAVLO *crawls under the covers of his bunk.*)

SGT. TOWER. Now I'm gonna tell you gen'l'men how you find you way when you lost. You better listen up. What you do, you find the North Star and the North Star show you true north accurate all year round. You look for the Big Dipper and there are two stars at the end a that place in the stars that look like the bowl on the dipper and they called the pointer. They them two stars at where the water would come out the dipper if it had some water and out from them on a straight line you gonna see this big damn star and that the North Star and it show you north and once you know that, gen'-l'men, you can figure the rest. You ain't lost no more.

MEN. (*From the darkness.*) YESSSS, SERGEANT! (*And entering to position themselves for next scene.*)

SGT. TOWER. I hope so. I do hope so. . . . (PIERCE, PARKER, OTHERS, *set up card game on footlocker.*)

KRESS. (*Passing bunk where* PAVLO *is a lump beneath his blanket.*) I wonder what the fuckin' chimney shittin' shit is doin' now? (HINKLE *settles curiously on the bunk next to* PAVLO.)

PARKER. You gonna see me, Pierce? (*Talking, if necessary, even as they set the card game up.*)

PIERCE. And raise you.

PARKER. Ten ta one, he's under there jerking off!

HINKLE. (*Bending near to* PAVLO.) No, no, he's got this paper bag and everything smells funny. Y'all some kind of acrobat, Hummel?

KRESS. He's got some chick's bicycle seat in a bag, man.

HINKLE. And the noises he's makin'.

PIERCE. Poor pathetic motherfucker.

KRESS. He ain't pathetic.

PIERCE. He is too.

PARKER. Under there pounding his pud.

KRESS. You musta not seen many pathetic people, you think he's pathetic.

PIERCE. I seen plenty.

PARKER. Call.

PIERCE. Full Boat. Jacks and threes! (*Laying down his cards.*)

PARKER. Jesus Goddamn Christ.

HINKLE. I was wonderin' can ah look in you all's bag, Hummel? (*Reaching under the blankets for the bag.*)

PARKER. Jesus Goddamn Christ.

HINKLE. Ohhhh . . . it's . . . you been sniffin' airplane glue. . . . (*And he laughs, "Ha, Ha, Ha," turns toward the others.*) Hummel's been sniffin' airplane glue.

KRESS. (*From his bed.*) ATTAWAY TO GO, HUMMEL.

HINKLE. An' where's all the aspirins . . . ? (*Holding the bottle.*)

PAVLO. Tum-tum, Pavlo.

HINKLE. You all kiddin' me.

PAVLO. No.

HINKLE. Y'all ate 'em?

PAVLO. Yeah!

HINKLE. Hey, y'all. . . . (*To* PAVLO.) Was it full? (PAVLO, *attempting to sit up, flops back down.*)

PAVLO. Tippy top.

HINKLE. Hummel just ate— (*Examining the bottle.*) 100 aspirins. Hummel just ate 'em.

KRESS. Attaway to go, Hummel.

PARKER. Nighty-night.

HINKLE. (*Moving toward* PIERCE.) Won't it hurt him, Pierce?

KRESS. Kill him probably.

PARKER. Hopefully.

KRESS. Hinkle, ask him did he use chocolate syrup?

HINKLE. He's breathin' kinda funny, Pierce, don't you think?

KRESS. Hummel does everything funny.

PIERCE. (*Beginning to deal.*) Five cards, gen'l'men; jacks or better.

HINKLE. Pierce.

PIERCE. Hummel, you stop worryin' that boy. Tell him no headache big enough in the world, you're gonna take a hundred aspirins. (*Slight pause:* KRESS *begins imitating* PAVLO's *odd breathing.*) How come everybody's all the time bustin' up my good luck?

BURNS. Shit, man, he took a hundred aspirins, he wouldn't be breathing period.

RYAN. Sounds like a goddamn tire pump.

BURNS. Hummel, TEN HUT!

PIERCE. Hummel, you just jivin' cause you don't know what else to do or did you eat them pills?

BURNS. Tryin' to blow himself up like a balloon . . . drift away. Float outa the fort.

(PARKER *begins to imitate* KRESS *imitating* PAVLO'S *breathing.*)

RYAN. He's fakin', man.

BURNS. How you know?

RYAN. They'd kill you like a bullet.

HINKLE. Get over here, Pierce! (*Throwing down his cards,* PIERCE *goes to the bed.*)

KRESS. How come the army don't throw him out, Parker?

PARKER. Army likes weird people, Kress.

KRESS. I hate weird people.

PARKER. Sure you do.

KRESS. Weird chimney-shittin' friendless, gutless cheatin'—

(PIERCE *is examining* PAVLO. *And* PAVLO *makes a sound and then begins to cough, to sputter.*)

PIERCE. (*Realizing what is true.*) NOOO! NOT IN MY SQUAD, YOU MOTHER, GET UP. (*He is trying to get* PAVLO *to his feet, the* FIRST SOLDIER *is helping.*) YOU SILLY SONOFABITCH. We got to walk him. (PAVLO *is feebly resisting, saying, "no, no."*) Hinkle, double-time-it over the orderly room.

HINKLE. (*Backing for the door.*) Right.

PIERCE. Tell 'em we got a guy over here took a hundred aspirins, they should get an ambulance.

HINKLE. (*Turning to head for the door.*) Right.

KRESS. Hinkle!

HINKLE. (*Hesitating, turning back, to face* KRESS.) Yeh!

or, man? Who you see? That ain't no Pavlo Hummel.
oo, man. That somebody else. An' he somethin' else.
h, you goin' out on the street, they gonna see you.
ell tellin' you and Ardell know. You back on the block
you goin' out struttin'. An' they gonna cry when they
you. You so pretty, baby, you gonna make 'em cry.
tell me you name, you pretty baby!
AVLO. (*Snapping to attention.*) PAVLO MOTHER-
MPIN' HUMMEL!

BLACKOUT

KRESS. Pick me up a Coke on your way back. (*And*
HINKLE *leaves.*)

PIERCE. Hold him steady, I think we oughta get him
outside, more air. (*Working with the aid of another*
SOLDIER.)

ARDELL. (*Standing over near the base of the platform.*)
Pavlo. You gonna have ambulances and sirens and all
kinds a good shit. Ain't you somethin'? It gonna be a
celebration. C'mon over here. (*As if his voice draws
them, they lug* PAVLO *toward the tower, walking him;
they lay him down, remove all clothes from him but his
underwear and T shirt.*) PAVLO. Look at you. You got
people runnin' around like a bunch a fools. That what
you wanted? Yeah, that what you want! They sayin,'
"Move him. Lift him. Take his shirt off." They walkin'
you around in the air. They all thinkin' about you, anyway. But what you doin' but cryin'? You always think
you signifyin' on everybody else, but all you doin' is
showin' your own fool self. You don't know nothin' about
showboatin,' Pavlo. You hear me? Now you get on up
off that floor. You don't get up, man, I blow a motherfuckin' whistle up side a you head. I blow it loud.
YOU THINK YOU GOT A MOTHERFUCKIN'
WHISTLE IN YOUR BRAIN! (PIERCE *and the other*
SOLDIER *have turned away, frozen.* PAVLO *has jumped.
Everything he does is performed in the manner of a person alone: as if* ARDELL *is a voice in his head. The light
perhaps suggests this.* KRESS, *all others, are frozen as
when* HINKLE *left.*) I'm tellin' you how to be. That right.
(PAVLO *slumps back down.*) Ohhh, don't act so bad; you
actin', man. What you expect, you go out get you head
smokin' on all kinds a shit sniffin' that goddamn glue
then fallin' down all over yourself. Man, you lucky you
alive, carryin' on like that. (PAVLO *is doubled over.*)
Ain't doin' you no good you wish you dead, 'cause you
ain't, man. You know you do. Get on up. (PAVLO *takes
a deep breath and stands.*) You go on in the latrine now,
get you a Bromo, you wash off you face . . . (PAVLO

exits.) Then get you ass right back out here. And you don't need no shave, man, you ain't got no beard no ways. (*He sees* PAVLO's *uniform lying on the floor.*) What kinda shit this? Your poor ole sarge see this, he sit down on the ground and he cry, man. Poor ole Sarge, he work himself like he crazy tryin ta teach you so you can act like a man. An' what you do? (*Turning suddenly toward the door through which* PAVLO *exited.*) PAVLO! You diddlin' in there, you take this long. And you bring out you other uniform. We gonna shape you up. (PAVLO *enters carrying military dress uniform in clothing bag, which he hangs on the tower.*) It daytime, man, you goin' out struttin'. You goin' out standin' tall. You tear it open. Trousers first, man. Dig 'em out. (PAVLO, *having selected the trousers, moves as if to put them on.*) NOOOO! Damnit, ain't you got no sense at all? (*He has rushed to* PAVLO, *lifted the trouser bottoms from off the floor.*) You drag 'em all over the floor like that, man, they gonna look like shit. Get up on this footlocker! (*Pulling a footlocker into place.* PAVLO, *stands on the footlocker, puts on the trousers. Now* PIERCE *and the other* SOLDIER *move to help* PAVLO *dress. All is ease and grace now.*) That right, that it. Make 'em look like they got no notion at all what it like ta be dirty. Be clean, man. Yeh. (PIERCE *has moved before* PAVLO, *pulling down on the cuffs, pulling the crease tight.*) Now the shirt. (*It is a ritual now.* PAVLO *must exert no effort whatsoever as he is transformed. Everything is done for him.*) Lemme look you brass over. (SOLDIER *moves to the jacket.*) Ain't too bad. It do. Lemme just touch 'em up a little. You put on you tie. Make you a big knot. Big knot make you look tall. (*He is brushing with his handkerchief at the brass.*) Where you boots? (*And finished with the jacket,* PIERCE *and other* SOLDIER *move to boots.*) Where you boots? An' you got some shades? Lemme get you some shades. (*Walking backwards.*) And tuck that tie square. Give her little loop she come off you throat high and pretty. (*As* ARDELL *exits, beginning*

the song, PAVLO *sits on the footloc the other* SOLDIER *kneel to each put* PAVLO *sits with his back to audienc*
. . . HEE . . . HAW . . . IF I H
MEN.
    IF I HAD A LOWER I.Q.
        (*All* MEN, KRESS *and* ALL, *s*
ARDELL.
    I COULD BE A SERGEANT
MEN.
    I COULD BE A SERGEANT
        (*Across the back of the stage*
ARDELL.
    LORD HAVE MERCY, I'M S
        (*The* TWO MEN *do an intrica*
MEN.
    IT FOUR MORE WEEKS T
        THROUGH.
        (*The* TWO MEN *spin and sto*
ARDELL. You gonna be over, mar
(*Re-entering with the sunglasses a now fully dressed.*) You gonna be tl
eatin' cheese. (ARDELL *moves abou him, guiding him toward the towe climb and stand upon and then* ARDI
him.) OVER, BABY! Ardell can ma
startin' ta look good now; you finis
the fattest rat, man; eatin' the fines
good company, you wear that uniforr
on the street, people know you, the
Somebody else say, "Man, he strai
Somebody else say, "That boy got
Pavlo, you gonna be over, man. Yo
fat rat, eatin' cheese, down on hi
doffin' his red cap, sayin' "Yes, Ma
there. (*They are both atop the towe hind* PAVLO *and gesturing outwa stands. He has sunglasses on.*) W

ACT TWO

CAPTAIN *and* SGT. TOWER *are* U., *facing out.* PAVLO *still*
stands on the tower, with other SOLDIERS *in forma-*
tion below. MICKEY, PAVLO'S *brother, stands* D.,
looking out as if into a mirror, combing his hair.

CAPTAIN. As we enter now the final weeks of your basic
training, I feel a certain obligation as your company commander to speak to you of the final purpose of what has
gone on here. Normally this is more difficult to make
clear. Pleiku, Vietnam, is the purpose of what we have
done here. A few nights ago, mortar and machine gun
fire in a sneak attack in the highlands killed 9 Ameri-
cans and wounded 140 serving at our camp there in
Pleiku. In retaliation, a bombing of the North has begun
and it will continue until the government of Hanoi,
battered and reeling, goes back to the North.

SGT. TOWER. Company, fall out.

(*And the* TROOPS *scatter. MUSIC starts from* MICKEY'S
radio. PAVLO *descends. Picks up duffle bag, AWOL*
bag.)

PAVLO. Hey, Mickey, it's me. I'm home! (MICKEY, *in*
T shirt, slacks, shoes, combs hair.) It's me. I'm home, I'm
home, I'm home.

MICKEY. Whata you say, huh? Hey, hey, what happened? You took so long. You took a wrong turn, huh?
Missed your stop and now you come home all dressed up
like a conductor. What happened? You were down in
that subway so long they put you to work? Huh? Man,
you look good though; you look good. Where were you
again?

PAVLO. Georgia.

MICKEY. Hot as a bitch, right?

PAVLO. No. Cold.

MICKEY. In Georgia?

PAVLO. Yeh, it was real cold; we used to hide out in the furnace room every damn chance we ever got.

MICKEY. Hey, you want a drink? Damn, that don't make much sense, does it?

PAVLO. What?

MICKEY. They send you to Georgia for the winter and it's like a witch's tit. Can you imagine that? A witch's tit? Eeeeeeggggggg. Put ice on your tongue. That ever happens to me, man, I'd turn in my tool. Ain't you gonna ask about the ole lady? How's she doin' and all that, 'cause she's doin' fine. Pickin' and plantin' daisies. Doin' fine. (*And* PAVLO *laughs softly, shaking his head, taking the drink* MICKEY *has made him.*) Whatsa matter? You don't believe yo-yos can be happy? Psychotics have fun, man. You oughta know that.

PAVLO. I just bet she's climbin' some kinda wall. Some kinda wall and she's pregnant again, she thinks, or you are or me or somebody.

MICKEY. Noo, man, noo, it's everybody else now. Only non-family.

PAVLO. (*Laughing, loudly.*) THAT'S ME AND YOU! NON-FAMILY MOTHERFUCKERS!

MICKEY. All the dogs and women of the world!

PAVLO. Yeh, yeh, all the guys in the barracks used to think I was a little weird so I'd—

MICKEY. —you are a little weird— (*Slight pause.*)

PAVLO. Yeh, yeh, I'd tell 'em, "You think I'm weird, you oughta see my brother, Mickey. He don't give a big rat's ass for nothin' or nobody."

MICKEY. And did you tell 'em about his brains, too? And his wit and charm. The way his dick hangs to his knees—about his 18 thou a year? Did you tell 'em all that sweet shit?

PAVLO. They said they hoped you died of all you got.

MICKEY. (*Has been dressing throughout: shirt, tie,*

jacket.) How come the troops were thinkin' you weird? You doin' that weird stuff again. You say "Georgia" and "the army." For all I know you been down town in the movies for the last three months and you bought that goddamn uniform at some junk shop.

PAVLO. I am in the army.

MICKEY. How do I know?

PAVLO. I'm tellin' you.

MICKEY. But you're a fuckin' liar; you're a fuckin' myth maker.

PAVLO. I gotta go to Vietnam, Mickey.

MICKEY. Vietnam don't even exist.

PAVLO. I gotta go to it.

MICKEY. Arizona, man; that's where you're goin' Wyoming.

PAVLO. Look at me! I'm different! I'm different than I was! (*This is with fury and there is a pause.*) I'm not the same anymore. I was an asshole. I'm not an asshole anymore. I'm not an asshole anymore! (*Slight pause.*) I came here to forgive you. I don't need you anymore.

MICKEY. You're a goddamn cartoon, you know that.

PAVLO. (*Rapidly. A rush of words.*) I'm happier now than I ever was, I got people who respect me. Lots of 'em. There was this guy Kress in my outfit. We didn't hit it off . . . and he called me out . . . he was gonna kill me, he said. Everybody tried to stop me because this guy had hurt a lot of people already and he had this uncle who'd taught him all about fightin' and this uncle had been executed in San Quentin for killing people. We went out back of the barracks. It went on and on, hitting and kicking. It went on and on; all around the barracks. The crowd right with us. And then . . . all of a sudden . . . this look came into his eye . . . and he just stopped . . . and reached down to me and hugged me. He just hugged and hugged me. And that look was in all their eyes. All the soldiers. I don't need you anymore, Mickey. I got real brothers now.

MICKEY. You know . . . if my father hadn't died, you wouldn't even exist.

PAVLO. No big thing! We got the same mother; that's shit enough. I'm gonna shower and shave, O.K.? Then we can go out drinkin'.

MICKEY. All those one-night stands. You ever think of that? Ghostly pricks. I used to hear 'em humpin' the ole whore. I probably had my ear against the wall the night they got you goin'.

PAVLO. (After a slight silence.) You seen Joanna lately?

MICKEY. Joanna?

PAVLO. Joanna. My ole girl. I thought maybe she probably killed herself and it was in the papers. You know, on account of my absence. But she probably did it in secret.

MICKEY. No doubt.

PAVLO. No doubt.

MICKEY. Ain't she the one who got married? I think the ole lady tole me Joanna got married and she was gonna write you a big letter all about it. Sure she was. Anyway, since we're speaking of old girls and pregnant people, I've got to go to this little party tonight. Got a good new sweet young thing and she thinks I'm better than her daddy. I've had a run a chicks lately you wouldn't believe, Pavlo. They give away ass like Red Cross girls dealin' out donuts. I don't understand how I get half a what I get. Oh yeah, old lady comes and goes around here. She's the same old witch.

PAVLO. I'm gonna go see Joanna. I'll call her up. Use the magic fuckin' phone to call her up.

MICKEY. I'll give you a call later on.

PAVLO. I'll be out, man. I'll be out on the street.

MICKEY. You make yourself at home. (Exiting.)

(And SOLDIERS appear far U., marching forward as ARDELL, off to the side, counts cadence, and other SOLDIERS appear at various points about the stage.)

ARDELL.
HUT . . . HOO . . . HEE . . .

SGT. TOWER. (*Entering as* PAVLO, *glancing at him,
wanders off.*)
SAW SOME STOCKIN'S ON THE
STREET. . . .

MEN.
WISHED I WAS BETWEEN THOSE FEET.

SGT. TOWER.
WISHED I WAS BETWEEN THOSE FEET.
HONEY, HONEY, DON'T YOU FROWN.

MEN.
I LOVE YOU DRUNK AND LAYIN' DOWN.

SGT. TOWER.
STANDIN' TALL AND LOOKIN' GOOD. WE
BELONG IN HOLLYWOOD.

(*Atop the tower as the* MEN *come to a stomping
halt.*)

MEN.
WE BELONG IN HOLLYWOOD.

SGT. TOWER. Take five, gen'l'men, but the smoking
lamp is not lit.

(PAVLO *is there, off to the side, disheveled, carrying a
pint whiskey bottle. He undresses, speaking his
anger, throwing his uniform down.*)

PAVLO. Stupid fuckin' uniform. Miserable hunk a green
shit. Don't we go to good bars—why don't you work for
me? And there's this really neat girl there sayin' to me
how do I like bein' a robot? How do I like bein' one in
a hundred million robots all marchin' in a row? Don't
anybody understand about uniforms? I ain't no robot.
You gotta have braid . . . ribbons and patches all about
what you did. I got nothin'. What's so complicated? I
look like nothin' 'cause I done nothin'. (*In his T shirt
and underwear, he kneels now with the bottle.*)

SGT. TOWER. Gen'l'men, you best listen up real close

now even though you restin'. Gonna tell you little bit about what you do you comin' through the woods, you find a man wounded in his chest. You gotta seal it off. That wound workin' like a valve, pullin' in air makin' pressure to collapse that man's lung; you get him to breathe out and hold his breath. You apply the metal foil side a the waterproof wrapping of the first aid dressing, tie it off. Gonna hafta tie it extra; you use your poncho, his poncho, you get strips a cloth. You tear up you own damn shirt, I don't care. You let that boy have his lung. You let him breathe. AM I UNDERSTOOD?

MEN. YES, SERGEANT!

SGT. TOWER. FALL IN. DISMISSED!

(*The* TROOPS *go, leaving* PAVLO *alone, in his underwear, near or on the bed.*)

PAVLO. I wanna get laid . . . , bed . . . bottle. (*Pause.*) I wanna get laid! I wanna get laid, phone! You goddamn stuck-up motherin' phone. Need a piece of ass, bed. Lemme walk on over to that phone. Lemme crawl on over to that phone. Lemme get there. Gonna outflank you. Goddamn army ant. Tha's right. Tha's right. Hello. (*Dialing now, he has crawled to the phone.*) This is Pavlo, Joanna, hello. Certainly of course. I'd be glad to screw your thingy with my thingy. BSZZZZZZZ . . . BBBBBBBBZZZZZZZZZZZZZZ . . . BBBZZZ . . .

WOMAN. (*On the phone.*) Hello?

PAVLO. BBBZZZZZZZZZZZZZZZZZZZZZZ . . .

WOMAN. Hello?

PAVLO. Little bitty creature . . . hello, hello. . . .

WOMAN. Who is this?

PAVLO. Hollering . . . hollering . . . poor creature . . . locked inside, can't get out, can't—

WOMAN. Pavlo?

PAVLO. Do you know me? Yes. Yes, it is me, Pavlo. Pavlo Hummel . . . Joanna. . . . And I am calling to ask how can you have lived to this day away from me?

WOMAN. Pavlo, listen.

PAVLO. Yes. I am. I do.

WOMAN. This isn't Joanna.

PAVLO. What?

WOMAN. This is Mrs. Sorrentino, Pavlo. Joanna isn't here.

PAVLO. What?

WOMAN. I said, "Joanna isn't here," Pavlo. This is her mother; may I have her call you?

PAVLO. What?

WOMAN. I said, "May I have her call you?" Or did you just call to say hello?

PAVLO. Who is this?

WOMAN. Pavlo, what's wrong with you?

PAVLO. Who are you? I don't know who this is. You get off the line, goddamnit, you hear me, or I'll report you to the telephone company. I'll report you to Bell Telephone. And G.E., too. And the Coke Company and General Motors. (*The* WOMAN *hangs up the phone.*) You'll be hurtin', baby. I report you to all those people. Now you tell me where she is. Where is she?

(*And behind him a LIGHT pops on, a table lamp. His* MOTHER, *a small, dark-haired woman, plump, fashionably dressed. She has been there all the while sitting in the dark, listening, visible only as a figure in a chair. She begins to speak almost at the same instant that the LIGHT goes on. At first tentative, she then gains confidence, gathers speed, tells her story as if she is simply thinking it.*)

MRS. HUMMEL. In Stratford, Connecticut, Pavlo. Pregnant more than likely. Vomiting in the morning. Yes . . . trying . . . to . . . get . . . rid of . . . it. . . . Hello, Pavlo . . . I wrote you that . . . I wrote you. (*Silence.*) Hello . . . Pavlo. I wrote you she was married. Why are you calling? Why? (*Silence.*) Pavlo? Listen, are you finished on the phone and could we talk a minute? I don't want to interrupt . . . I only have a few . . . few things to say. They won't take long. I've been working since you've been gone. Did you know? Doing quite well. Quite well indeed. In a department store. Yes. One of the smaller ones. Yes. And we had an awful, awful shock there the other day and that's what I want to tell you about. There's a woman, Sally Kelly, and Ken was her son, in the army like you now and he went overseas last August. Well, I talked to Sally when I went in at noon and she was in the lunch room writing a little card to Ken and she let me read it. She knew that you were in the army so she said she was sure I knew the way it was consolation to write a little note. Then about 5:45, I was working on the shoes and I saw two army officers come up the escalator and talk to one of the other clerks. I never gave them another thought and at 6:00 o'clock Sally came through and went down the escalator and made a remark to me and laughed a little and went on down. In about fifteen more minutes, I was waiting on a lady and she said to me, "Isn't that terrible about the lady's son who works downstairs?" I said, "Who?" She said, "The lady who works at your candy department just got word her son was killed in Vietnam." Well, I was really shook when I heard that and I said, "Oh, you must be mistaken. She just went downstairs from her supper hour and I talked to her and she was fine." She said, "Well, that's what I heard on the main floor." Well, I went right to the phone and called the reception desk and they said it was true. This is what happened, this is what I want to tell you. The officers had gone to Sally's house but no one was home so they talked to the neighbors and found out Sally worked at the store. So they went up to our receptionist and asked for our manager. He wasn't in so they asked for one of the men and Tommy Bottle came and they told him they needed his help because they had to tell one of the employees that her son was killed in Vietnam. Tommy really got shook as you can imagine and he took the officers to

Mr. Brenner's office and closed the door. While they were in there, Sally came out of the lunch room and came downstairs. Joyce, the girl who is the receptionist knew by this time and Sally laughed when she went by and said that she better get to work or something like that. Joyce said later on that she could hardly look at her. Anyway, Tommy called the floorman from first floor to come up and he told him what had happened and then he had to go back down to first floor and tell Sally she was wanted in Tommy's office. She said, "Oh, boy, what have I done now?" By the time she got to the fourth floor, the office door was open and she saw the two army men and said, "Oh, dear God, not Kenny." (*Pause.*) A mother . . . and her children should be as a tree and her branches . . . A mother spends . . . but she gets . . . change. You think me a fool . . . don't you? There are many who do. (*Pause.*) He joined to be a mechanic and they transfered him to Infantry and he was killed on December first. So you see . . . I know what to expect. I know . . . what you're trying to do.

PAVLO. Who . . . was . . . my father? Where is he?

MRS. HUMMEL. You know that.

PAVLO. No, I want you to tell me.

MRS. HUMMEL. I've already told you.

PAVLO. No, where is he now? What did he look like?

MRS. HUMMEL. I wrote it all in a letter. I put it all in an envelope, I sealed it, mailed it.

PAVLO. I never got it.

MRS. HUMMEL. I think you did.

PAVLO. No!

MRS. HUMMEL. No, you had many fathers, many men, movie men, filmdom's great—all of them, those grand old men of yesteryear, they were your father. The Fighting 76th, do you remember, oh, I remember, little Jimmy, what a tough little mite he was, and how he leaped upon that grenade, did you see, my god what a glory, what a glorious thing with his little tin hat.

PAVLO. My real father!

MRS. HUMMEL. He was like them, the ones I showed you in movies, I pointed them out.

PAVLO. What was his name?

MRS. HUMMEL. I've told you.

PAVLO. No. What was his name? I don't know what it was.

MRS. HUMMEL. Is it my fault you've forgotten?

PAVLO. You never told me.

MRS. HUMMEL. I did. I whispered it in your ear. You were three. I whispered the whole thing in your ear!

PAVLO. Lunatic!

MRS. HUMMEL. Nooooo!

PAVLO. Insane hideous person!

MRS. HUMMEL. (*Slight pause.*) I've got to go to bed now. I have to get my rest. (*Her back is turned. She is walking.*)

PAVLO. I picked this girl up in this bar tonight and when I took her home and got her to the door and kissed her, her tongue went into my mouth. I thought that meant she was going to let me in to her apartment. "Don't get hurt," she said, "and get in touch when you get back, I'd love to see you." She knew I was going overseas, did you? And then the door was shut and all I wanted to say was, "What are you doing sticking your tongue in my mouth and then leaving me, you goddamn stuck-up motherin' bitch?" But I didn't say anything.

MRS. HUMMEL. Yes . . . well . . . I'll see you in the morning . . . Pavlo . . . (*And she leaves.*)

ARDELL. (*Who has been watching.*) Oh, man, how come? You wanted to get laid, how come you didn't do like the ole Sarge told you steada gettin' all tore up with them walkin' blues? Take you a little money, the old Sarge say, roll it up long ways, put it in your fly, man, so it stickin' out. Then go on walkin' up and down the street that green stickin' right outa your fly. You get laid. You got that money stickin' outa your fly, you get laid. You get your nut! How come you didn't do that?

OFFICER. (*Who has been standing on rear platform at Parade Rest.*) And the following will depart conus 12 August 1966 for the Republic of Vietnam or assignment to the 23rd Field Hospital. Tnomas. Simpson. Horner. Hinkle. Hummel.

PAVLO. I don't wanna be no medic!

(*And the BAR MUSIC starts, YEN and OLDER VIET-NAMESE WOMAN entering from one side of the stage, BRISBEY calling from the other and then entering, his bed on wheels pushed onstage by two SOLDIERS, while ARDELL has hauled off the footlocker on which the phone had set, showing a pile of clothes, PAVLO's jungle fatigues which he immediately starts getting into. YEN is at the bar. All this happens nearly simultaneously. BRISBEY calls "Pavlo," YEN entering, MUSIC starting.*)

YEN. Hey, G.I. cheap Charlie, you want one more beer?

JONES. (*Offstage.*) One bomniba, one beer.

BRISBEY. Pavlo.

YEN. (*As JONES in a bright colored walking suit enters.*) EEEEEEaaaaaa? What you talk? One bomniba, one beer. Same—same, huh? I no stand. What you want?

JONES. (*Pursuing her, both are playing yet both have real anger.*) You gimme boucoup now?

YEN. Boucoup what? I don't know what you want. Crazy G.I., you dinky dow.

BRISBEY. PAVLO!

PAVLO. (*Who is and has been dressing into jungle fatigues.*) I'm in the can, Brisbey, I'll be there in a minute.

ARDELL. He be there, Brisbey.

JONES. You got lips as fat as mine, you know that, ho?

YEN. Toi cum biet!

JONES. Shit, you don't know.

YEN. Shit. I can say, too. I know. Shit. (*And he is*

reaching for her.) No. We fini. Fini. You no talk me no more, you numba fuckin' ten. (*And she bounces away to sit on a crate and look at sheet music, as* BRISBEY *speaks to* PAVLO.)

BRISBEY. Do you know, Pavlo? I saw the metal point of that mine sticking up from the ground just under my foot—I said, "That's a mine. I'm stepping on a mine." And my foot went right on down and I felt the pin sink and heard the first small . . . pop. I jumped . . . like a fool. And up she came right outa the ground. I hit at it with my hand as if to push it away, it came up so slow against my hand. . . . Steel . . . bits . . . of dirt . . .

PAVLO. I'm off duty now, Brisbey. (*Having listened reluctantly.*)

ARDELL. Ole Brisbey got himself hit by a Bouncin' Betty. That a kind of land mine; you step on it, she jump up to about right here, (*Indicating his waist.*) then she blow you in half. That why she got that name. Little yellow man dug a hole, put it in, hoped he'd come around. He an old man, damn near; got seventeen years in the army; no legs no more, no balls, one arm.

(*A* SMALL VIETNAMESE BOY *comes almost running across stage to grab* PAVLO's *hand and guide him into the WHOREHOUSE, BAR area, and leave him there.*)

BOY. HEY, G.I. SHOW YOU NUMBA ONE!

PAVLO. Hey, what's goin' on? (*To* JONES *who is sitting there drinking a beer.*)

JONES. What's happenin', man?

MAMASAN. (*The elderly Vietnamese* WOMAN, *returning.*) Hello, hello! You come my house, I am glad. Do you want a beer? I have. Do you want a girl? I have. Number one girl. Number one. You want?

PAVLO. (*Pointing to* MAMASAN.) You?

MAMASAN. No, no, I am Mamasan. But I have many girl. You see, maybe you like. Maybe you want short time, huh? Maybe you want long time. I don't know, you tell me. All number one. (JONES *laughs*.)

JONES. Man, don't you believe that ole lady, you just gotta get on and ride. Like her. (*Indicating* YEN.) I been. And I'm restin' to go again; an' I don't think it any kinda numba one; but I been outa the world so *damn* long. I jus' close my eyes an' jive my own self— "That ain't no dead person," I say, "that ain't no dead Ho jus' 'cause she layin' so still. I saw her walk in here." I mean, man, they so screwed up over here. They got no nature. You understand me, Bro? They got no nature, these women. You—how long you been over here?

PAVLO. Not long; couple weeks.

JONES. You new then, huh?

PAVLO. Yeh.

JONES. You wanna go? (*Reaching out toward* YEN *who is across the room, calling to her*.) Hey, Ho! C'mon over here!

YEN. You talk me?

JONES. Yeh, baby, you, c'mon over here. You wanna go, man?

PAVLO. What about the V.D.? (*Taking a seat*.)

JONES. (*Big laugh*.) What about it?

YEN. (*Who, approaching, with a beer, has heard*.) I no have. I no sick. No. No sweat, G.I. You want short-time me, no sweat.

JONES. Shit, Ho, you insides rotten. You Vietnamee, ain't you? Vietnamee same-same V.D.

YEN. No! No sick. (*As* JONES *grabs her, pulls her near, then sets her down on* PAVLO's *lap*.) What you do? No.

JONES. (*Holding her in place*.) I'm jus' tryin' ta help you get some money, baby. I be you sportsman. Okay. (*She has stopped her struggle, is sitting nicely on* PAVLO's *lap*.) You just sit on down an' be nice on the man's lap, pretty soon, he ain't gonna be worried 'bout no V.D. If you jus' . . . sorta shift . . . (*Demonstrates*.) every now and then. Okay . . . (*She is still now and he turns*

his attention to PAVLO.) Now, lemme tell you 'bout it,
lemme tell you how it is. It be hot, man. I come from
Georgia, and it get hot in Georgia, but it ain't ever been
this kinda hot, am I lyin'? An' you gonna be here one
year and that three-hundred-sixty-five days, so you gonna
sweat, now do you think I'm lyin'?

PAVLO. I ain't never sweat so much. (*She has been
messing with him, rubbing under his shirt.*)

JONES. So that's what I'm sayin'. You gonna be here
and you gonna sweat. And you gonna be here and you
gonna get V.D. You worried about sweatin'? Ahhhhh.
You grinnin'. So I see I have made my meanin' clear.
(*She has been rubbing his thigh.*) How you feelin' now?
She kinda nice, huh? She kinda soft and nice.

PAVLO. Where you work? (JONES *laughs.*)

JONES. Don't you be askin' me where I work. That
ain't what you wanna know. I gotta get you straight,
my man, gotta get outa here, buy myself some supplies.
My ole Mom all the time tellin' me, "Don't you go near
that P.X. You get blown away for sure. Them V.C.'s
gotta wanna get that P.X."

PAVLO. (*To* YEN.) What's your name?

YEN. Name me Yen.

PAVLO. Name me Pavlo. Pavlo.

YEN. Paaa-blo.

PAVLO. How much?

JONES. Lord, she says his name, he loves her.

YEN. You want short-time. I ask Mamasan. (*She is
getting up, but* MAMASAN *has been watching.*)

MAMASAN. (*Approaching.*) O.K. O.K. Yen numba one.
I am happy. 500 peas.

JONES. Two hundred.

MAMASAN. She very beautiful.

JONES. Two-fifty.

MAMASAN. Four hundred; can do. No sweat.

JONES. Mamasan, who you think you jivin'?

MAMASAN. Yen boucoup boy friend! She very love!

JONES. Two-fifty.

MAMASAN. (*To* PAVLO.) Three hundred twenty. You, huh? Three hundred twenty.

JONES. Pavlo, give her three hundred, tell her things is tough at home, she don't know.

MAMASAN. (*As* PAVLO *hands her the money.*) No, no, I talk you three hundred twenty!

JONES. AND I TALK HIM THREE HUNDRED, MAMASAN, THREE HUNDRED.

MAMASAN. (*Softly, whiney, to* PAVLO.) G.I. You be nice; you give Mamasan ten peas more. G.I.? Ten peas very easy you!

PAVLO. (*To* JONES.) How much *is* ten peas, Man?

JONES. Eight cents, or about—

PAVLO. Eight cents! Eight cents. Over eight goddamn stupid cents I'm still standin' here!

JONES. Man, no! (*As* PAVLO *is giving more money to* MAMASAN.)

MAMASAN. (*Patting him on the back.*) Okay, okay. You numba one—

YEN. (*Taking* PAVLO *by the hand toward the bed.*) I show you.

JONES. (*As he leaves.*) Oh man, deliver me from these green troops; they makin' everybody fat but me.

(*The WHISTLE blows loudly, and the troops come roaring on and into formation for instructions; they face the tower.*)

SGT. TOWER. (*His voice booming.*) GEN'L'MEN! (*And his voice stops* PAVLO, *who comes to attention kneeling on the bed.* YEN *has jumped onto the bed. And as* SGT. TOWER *continues his speech, she unbuttons* PAVLO'S *pants, unbuttons his shirt, takes his pants down, all this as* SGT. TOWER *gives instructions. He is holding up a rifle.*) This an M-16 rifle, this the best you country got, now we got to make you good enough to have it. You got to have feelin' for it, like it a good woman to you, like it you arm, like it you rib. The command is *Right Shoulder . . . HARMS!* At the command, HARMS, raise and carry the rifle diagonally across the body, at the same time grasping it at the balance with the left hand, trigger guard in the hollow of the bone. Then carry the left hand, thumb and fingers extended to the small of the stock, and cut away smartly and everything about you, trainee, is at the position of attention. RIGHT SHOULDER. HARMS!

MEN. (*Performing it.*) 1—2—3—4. (PAVLO *also yells and performs the drill in pantomime.*)

SGT. TOWER. You got to love this rifle, gen'l'men, like it you pecker and you love to make love. You got to care about how it is and what can it do and what can it not do, what do it want and need. ORDER. HARMS!

MEN. 1—2—3—4.

SGT. TOWER. RIGHT SHOULDER. HARMS!

MEN. 1—2—3—4. (PAVLO *with them, yelling also.*)

CORPORAL. FORWARD HARCH! (PAVLO *pulls up his trousers and marches.*)

SGT. TOWER.

AIN'T NO USE IN GOIN' HOME . . .

MEN.

AIN'T NO USE IN GOIN' HOME . . .

(PAVLO'S *marching is joyous.*)

SGT. TOWER.

JODY GOT YOUR GAL AND GONE . . .

MEN.

JODY HUMPIN' ON AND ON . . .

(*Something of* PAVLO'S *making love to* YEN *is in his marching.*)

SGT. TOWER.

AIN'T NO USE IN GOIN' BACK . . .

MEN.

JODY GOT OUR CADILLAC.

CORPORAL.

LORD HAVE MERCY, I'M SO BLUE . . .

MEN.
IT TWO MORE WEEKS TILL I BE
        THROUGH.
CORPORAL. Count cadence, delayed cadence, count cadence—count.

(*And the* MEN, *performing delayed cadence, exit.* PAVLO
    *counts with them, marching away beside the bed,
    around the bed, leaping upon the bed as the count-
    ing comes to its loud end, and* BRISBEY, *who has
    been onstage in his bed, all this while, calls to*
    PAVLO.)

BRISBEY. Pavlo!
PAVLO. Just a second, Brisbey!
BRISBEY. Pavlo!
PAVLO. (*Crosses toward* BRISBEY.) Whatta you want,
Brisbey?
BRISBEY. Pavlo, can I talk to you a little?
PAVLO. Sure.
BRISBEY. You're a medic, right?
PAVLO. Yeh.
BRISBEY. But you're not a conscientious objector, are
you? So you got a rifle.
PAVLO. Sure.

(*During this scene,* PAVLO *busies himself with* BRISBEY'S
    *pulse and chart, straightening the bed, preparing the
    shot he must give* BRISBEY.)

BRISBEY. I like the feel of 'em. I like to hold 'em.
PAVLO. I'm not gonna get my rifle for you, Brisbey.
BRISBEY. Just as a favor.
PAVLO. No.
BRISBEY. It's the only pleasure I got any more.
PAVLO. Lemme give you a hypo; you got a visitor; you
can see him before you sleep.
BRISBEY. The egg that slept, that's what I am. You

think I look like an egg with a head? (PAVLO *is preparing the needle: there is a* FIGURE *off in the shadows.*) Or else I'm a stump. Some guys, they get hit, they have a stump. I am a stump.

PAVLO. What about your visitor; you wanna see him? (*And the* FIGURE *steps forward.*)

BRISBEY. Henry?

SGT. WALL. It's me, Brisbey, how you doin'? (*He is middle-aged, gray-haired, chunky.*)

BRISBEY. Henry, Henry, who was the first man 'round the world, Henry? That's what I want to know. Where's the deepest pit in the ocean? You carryin'? What do you have? .45? You must have a blade. Magellan. Threw out a rope. I ever tell you that story? Gonna go sleepy-bye. Been trying to get young Pavlo Hummel to put me away, but he prefers to break needles on me. How's the unit? You tell 'em I'll be back. You tell 'em, soon as I'm well, I'll be back.

SGT. WALL. I'm off the line . . . now, Brisbey. No more boonies. I'm in Supply now.

BRISBEY. Supply? What . . . do you supply? (*Slight pause, as if bewildered, thinking, yet with bitterness, with irony.*) If I promise to tell you the secret of life, Henry, will you slit my throat? You can do it while I'm sleeping.

PAVLO. Don't he just go on?

BRISBEY. Young Hummel here, tell him who you love. Dean Martin. Looks at ole Dino every chance he gets. And "Combat." Vic Morrow, man. Keeps thinkin' he's gonna see himself. Dino's cool, huh? Drunk all the time.

PAVLO. That's right.

BRISBEY. You fucking asshole. Henry. Listen. You ever think to yourself, "Oh, if only it wasn't Brisbey. I'd give anything. My own legs. Or one, anyway. Arms. Balls. Prick." Ever . . . Henry? (*Silence.*)

SGT. WALL. No.

BRISBEY. Good. Don't. Because I have powers I never

dreamed of and I'll hear you if you do, Henry, and I'll
take them. I'll rip them off you. (*Silence.*)

SGT. WALL. You'll be goin' home soon. I thought . . .
we could plan to get together. . . .

BRISBEY. Right. Start a softball team.

SGT. WALL. Jesus Christ, Brisbey, ain't you ever gonna
change? Ain't you ever gonna be serious about no—

BRISBEY. I have changed, Motherfucker. You blind or
somethin' askin' me if I changed? You get the fuck outa
here, hear me? (SGT. WALL *is leaving, having left a pint
of whiskey.*) You take a tree, you cut off its limbs, whatta
you got? You got a stump. A living, feeling, thinking
stump.

PAVLO. You're not a tree, Brisbey.

BRISBEY. And what terrible cruelty is that? Do you
know? There is responsibility. I want you to get me that
rifle. To save you from the sin of cruelty, Pavlo. (*As*
PAVLO *is moving with alcohol, cotton, to prepare the
shot.*) You are cruel, Pavlo . . . you and God. The both
of you.

PAVLO. Lemme do this, man.

BRISBEY. (*As* PAVLO *gives the shot.*) Do you know
. . . if you were to get the rifle, Pavlo, I'd shoot you
first. It's how you'll end up anyway. I'd save you time.
Get you home quicker. I know you, boy.

PAVLO. Shut up, man. Relax. . . .

BRISBEY. You've made me hate you.

PAVLO. I'm sorry. I didn't mean that to happen.

BRISBEY. No, no, you're not sorry. You're not. You're
glad it's me, you're glad it's not you. God's always glad
that way because it's never him, it's always somebody
else. Except that once. The only time we was ever gonna
get him, he tried to con us into thinkin' we oughta let
him go. Make it somebody else again. But we got through
all that shit he was talkin' and hung on and got him good
—fucked him up good—nailed him up good . . . just
once . . . for all the billion times he got us.

PAVLO. Brisbey, sometimes I don't think you know

what you're sayin'. (OFFICER *enters* U. L., *carrying clipboard*.) Grennel.

GRENNEL. Yes, sir. (*Appearing from the back, far* U.)

CAPTAIN. Go get me Hummel. He's down with Brisbey.

BRISBEY. I keep thinkin', Pavlo, 'bout this kid got his hand blown off, and he kept crawlin' round lookin' for his fingers. Couldn't go home without 'em, he said, he'd catch hell. No fingers. (PAVLO *shakes his head, mutters, "Brisbey, Brisbey."*) I keep think' about ole Magellan, sailin' round the world. Ever hear of him, Pavlo? So one day he wants to know how far under him to the bottom of the ocean. So he drops over all the rope he's got. 200 feet. It hangs down into a sea that must go down and down beyond its end for miles and tons of water. He's up there in the sun. He's got this little piece of rope dangling from his fingers. He thinks because all the rope he's got can't touch bottom, he's over the deepest part of the ocean. He doesn't know the real question. How far beyond all the rope you got is the bottom?

PAVLO. Brisbey, I'm gonna tell you somethin'. I tried to kill myself once. Honest to God. And it's no good. You understand me. I don't know what I was thinkin' about. I mean, you understand it was a long time ago and I'd never been laid yet or done hardly anything, but I have since and it's fantastic. I just about blew this girl's head off, it was fantastic, but if I'd killed myself, it'd never 'a' happened. You see what I'm saying, Brisbey? Somethin' fantastic might be comin' to you.

GRENNEL. (*Entering*.) Hummel. Man, the captain wants to see you.

PAVLO. Captain Miller? Captain Miller! (*Leaving*.)

BRISBEY. Pavlo!

GRENNEL. How you doin', Brisbey? (*As he wheels* BRISBEY *off*.)

PAVLO. (*Rushing up to the* CAPTAIN, *standing with his clipboard*.) Sir. Pfc Hummel reporting as ordered.

CAPTAIN. Good afternoon, Hummel.

PAVLO. Good afternoon, sir.

CAPTAIN. Are you smiling, Hummel?

PAVLO. Excuse me, sir.

CAPTAIN. Your ten-forty-nine says you're not happy at all; it says you want a transfer out of this unit because you're ashamed to serve with us. I was wondering how could you be ashamed and smiling simultaneously, Hummel.

PAVLO. I don't know, sir.

CAPTAIN. That's not a very good answer.

PAVLO. No, sir.

CAPTAIN. Don't you think what you're doing here is important? You helped out with poor Brisbey, didn't you?

PAVLO. Yes, sir.

CAPTAIN. That's my point, Hummel, there are people alive who would be dead if you hadn't done your job. Those invalids you care for, you feed them when they can't, you help them urinate, defecate, simple personal things they can't do for themselves but would die without. Have you asked any one of them if they think what you are doing is important or not, or if you should be ashamed?

PAVLO. Yes, sir . . . more or less. But . . . I . . . just . . . think I'd be better off in squad duty.

(*Distant firing and yelling are heard to which NEITHER the* CAPTAIN *nor* PAVLO *responds. There is a quality of echo to the sounds and then there is a clattering and a young Negro Pfc appears at the opposite side of the stage in full combat gear except for his helmet which is missing. He has come a few steps onto the stage and he crouches.*)

SOLDIER. Damn, baby, why that ole Sarge gotta pick on me?

PAVLO. I'm regular army, sir; I'm going to extend my tour.

CAPTAIN. You like it here, Hummel?

SOLDIER. Damn that ole Sarge. I run across that field I get shot sure as hell. (*He breathes.*) Lemme count to five. Lemme do it on 5. (*As he tenses, preparing.*)

CAPTAIN. How many days left in your tour, Hummel?

SOLDIER. Lemme do it like track and field.

PAVLO. I enlisted because I wanted to be a soldier, sir, and I'm not a soldier here. Four nights ago on perimeter guard, I tried to set up fields of fire with the other men in the bunker—do you know what I mean, sir? Designating who would be responsible for what sector of terrain in case of an attack? And they laughed at me; they just sat on the bunker and talked all night and they didn't stay low and they didn't hide their cigarettes when they smoked or anything.

SOLDIER. FIVE! (*And he runs, taking no more than two steps before a loud explosion hits and he goes down and hits, bounces and rolls onto his back, slamming his fist into the ground in outrage.*) DAMNIT! I KNEW IT! I KNEW IT! I KNEW IT!

CAPTAIN. You want the V.C. to come here?

PAVLO. I want to feel, sir, that I'm with a unit Victor Charlie considers valuable enough to want to get it. And I hope I don't have to kill anyone; and I hope I don't get killed.

SOLDIER. (*Still trying but unable to rise.*) Medic? Medic? Man, where you at? C'mon out here to me! Crawl on out here to me.

PAVLO. But maybe you can't understand what I'm saying, sir, because you're an R.O.T.C. officer and not O.C.S., sir.

CAPTAIN. You mean I'm not Regular Army, Hummel.

PAVLO. An R.O.T.C. officer and an O.C.S. officer are not the same thing.

CAPTAIN. Is that so, Hummel?

PAVLO. I think so, sir.

CAPTAIN. You want to get killed, don't you, Hummel?

PAVLO. No, sir. No.

CAPTAIN. And they will kill you, Hummel, if they get the chance. Do you believe that? That you will die if shot, or hit with shrapnel, that your arm can disappear into shreds, or your leg vanish, do you believe that, Hummel—that you can and will, if hit hard enough, gag and vomit and die . . . be buried and rot, do you believe yourself capable of that?

PAVLO. Yes, sir. I do.

SOLDIER. Nooooooo! (*Quick pause.*) Ohhh, shit, somebody don't help me, Charlie gonna come in here, cut me up, man. He gonna do me.

CAPTAIN. All right, Hummel.

SOLDIER. Oh, Lord, you get me outa here, I be good, man; I be good, no shit, Lord, I'm tellin' it.

CAPTAIN. All right . . . you're transferred. I'll fix it. (CAPTAIN *salutes, pivots, exits.*)

(PAVLO *moves to change into combat gear in darkening light. He finds the gear in a footlocker in the bar area. He exits.*)

SOLDIER. What's happenin'? I don't know what's happenin'! (*And the LIGHT GOES and the* SOLDIER *is alone in the jungle, in the center of silver; it is night, there are sounds.*) Hummel, c'mon. It's me, man; Parham, and I ain't jivin', mister. I been shot. I been truly shot. (*And he pauses, breathing, and raises his head to look down at himself.*) Ohhhh, look at me; ohhh, look at my poor stomach. Ohhhh, look at me, look at me. Oh, baby, stop it, stop bleedin', stop it, stop it; you my stomach, I'm talkin' to you, I'm tellin' you what to do, YOU STOP IT! (*His hands are pressing furiously down on his stomach. And he lies in silence for a moment: only his breathing.*) SOMEBODY GET ME A DUSTOFF! Dust off control, do you hear me? This here Pfc Jay Charles Johnson Parham. I am coordinates X-Ray Tango Foxtrot . . . Lima. . . . Do you hear me? I hurtin', baby . . .

hear me. Don't know what to do for myself . . . can't remember . . . don't know what it is gone wrong . . . requesting one med-evac chopper. . . . I am one litter patient; gunshot wounds; stomach. Area secure, c'mon hear me . . . this ole nigger . . . he gonna die.

FIRST V.C. Hello, G.I.

SOLDIER. Oh, no. Oh, no. No.

FIRST V.C. Okay. Okay. (*Very sing-song.*)

SECOND V.C. You number one.

SOLDIER. Get away from me! I talkin' to you, Charlie, you get away from me! You guys get away from me! MEDIC! ME—

(*They say "O.K., O.K." "You numba one" during above. And at a nod from the V.C. with the weapon, his partner has jumped forward into a sitting position at the head of the SOLDIER, one leg pinning down each shoulder, the hands, grasping under the chin, cocking the head back, stuffing a rag into the mouth. There are only the sounds of the struggle as the other V.C. approaches and crouches over the SOLDIER and holds a knife over the SOLDIER's eyes. He stares at it, his feet are moving slowly back and forth.*)

FIRST V.C. Numba one, you can see, G.I.? Airplane me . . . Vietnam. Have many bomb. Can do boom-boom, you 'stand! (*He moves the knife up and down.*) Same-same you, many friend me, fini. Where airplane now, G.I.? Where very gun? (*And he places the blade against the SOLDIER's chest and the SOLDIER, behind his gag, begins to howl and begins to flail his pinioned arms and beat his heels furiously upon the ground.*) Okay, okay . . . ! An di dow! (*Until the knife goes in and they rise up to stand over him as he turns onto his side and pulls himself into a knot as if to protect himself, knees tight to his chest, arms over his head. They unbuckle his pistol belt and take his flack vest and his bill-*)

fold from his pocket and are working at removing his shirt when they both straighten at a sound and then seize his fallen rifle and run to disappear. PAVLO appears, moving low, accompanied by a second American, RYAN.)

RYAN. Man, I'm tellin' you let's get outta here.

PAVLO. *(Pointing.)* No, no. There. *(He has a circular belt hooked over his shoulder. As he moves toward the body.)* Just look. *(RYAN is following.)* Hey, man . . . hey . . . *(He rolls him over.)* Ohhhhh . . . look at him.

RYAN. It's Parham.

PAVLO. Man, he's all cut. . . .

RYAN. Pavlo, let's out outta here . . . ! *(And he starts to move off.)* What the hell's it matter?

PAVLO. I'll carry him.

RYAN. I ain't worried about who has to carry him, for Crissake, I wanna get outta here. *(As PAVLO hands his rifle.)* I'm gonna hustle over there to the side there.

PAVLO. Nooooooo. . . .

RYAN. Give you some cover. *(And RYAN is gone, leaving PAVLO with the body.)*

(His task is as follows: The belt is placed under the buttocks of the man, one length above and along his back, the other below and across his legs so that two loops are formed—one on either side of the man. The carrier then lies down with his back to the dead man and he fits his arms through the two loops. He then grasps the man's left arm with his own right hand and rolls to his right so that the man rolls with him and is on his back: he then rises to one knee, keeping the body pressed tightly to his own. As PAVLO begins this task, ARDELL is there, appearing as RYAN departs.)

ARDELL. How many that make?

PAVLO. What's that?

ARDELL. Whatta you think, man? Dead bodies!

PAVLO. Who the hell's countin'?

ARDELL. Looookeeeee. Gettin' ta *beeeee bad!*

PAVLO. This one's nothin'. When they been out here a couple days, man, that's when it's interesting—you go to pick 'em up they fall apart in you hands, man. They're mud; pink mud; like turnin' over a log; all maggots and ants. You see Ryan over there hidin' in the bushes. I ain't hidin' in no bushes. And Parham's glad about that. They're all glad. Nobody wants to think he's gonna be let lay out here.

ARDELL. Ain't you somethin'!

PAVLO. I'm diggin' it, man. Blowin' people away. Cuttin' 'em down. Got two this afternoon I saw and one I didn't even see—just heard him out there jabberin' away— (*And he makes a sound mimicking a Vietnamese speaking.*) And I walked a good goddamn twenty rounds right over where it sounded like he was: he shut up his fucking face. It ain't no big thing.

ARDELL. Like bringing down a deer or dog.

PAVLO. Man, people's all I ever killed. Ohhhh, I feel you thinkin', "This poor boy don't know what he's doin'; don't know what he got into." But I do. I got a dead boy in my hands. In a jungle . . . the middle a the night. I got people maybe ten feet away, hidin'—they're gonna maybe cut me down the minute I move. And I'm gonna . . . (*During all this he has struggled to load the body like a pack on his back. Now he is rising, is on his knees.*) . . . take this dead thing back and people are gonna look at me when I do it. They're gonna think I'm crazy and be glad I'm with 'em. I'm diggin'— (*And the* VIETCONG *comes streaking out from his hiding place.*) Ryan, Ryan, Ryan! (*And the* VIETCONG, *without stopping, plunges the knife into* PAVLO'S *side and flees off.* PAVLO *falls, unable, because of the body on his back, to protect himself.*) What happened?

ARDELL. The blood goin' out a hole in your guts, man, turn you into water.

PAVLO. He hit me. . . .

ARDELL. TURN YOU INTO WATER! Blood goin' in the brain make you think—in you heart make you move, in your prick makes you hard, makes you come. YOU LETTIN' IT DROP ALL OVER THE GROUND!

PAVLO. I won't . . . I'll . . . noooooo . . . (*Trying to free himself of the body.*) Ryan . . .

ARDELL. The knowledge, comin', baby. I'm talkin' about what your kidney know, not your fuckin' fool's head. I'm talkin' about your skin and what it sayin', thin as paper. We melt; we tear and rip apart. Membrane, baby. Cellophane. Ain't that some shit!

PAVLO. I'll lift my arm. (*And he can't.*)

ARDELL. AIN'T THAT SOME SHIT.

PAVLO. Noooooo . . .

ARDELL. A bullet like this finger bigger than all your fuckin' life. Ain't this finger some shit!

PAVLO. RYAN.

ARDELL. I'm tellin' you.

PAVLO. Nooooo.

ARDELL. RYAN!

PAVLO. RYAN! (*As* RYAN *comes running on with a second* SOLDIER.)

ARDELL. Get on in here. (*They struggle to free* PAVLO *from the body. He flails, yelling in his panic as* SGT. TOWER *comes striding on and mounts the stairs to his tower.*)

PAVLO. Ryan, we tear. We rip apart. Ryan, we tear.

SGT. TOWER. (*As they move* PAVLO *off.*) You gonna see some funny shit, gen'l'men. You gonna see livin', breathin' people disappear. Walkin', talkin' buddies. And you gonna wanna kill and say their name. When you been in so many fights and you come out, you a survivor. It what you are and do. You survive.

(*A* BODY DETAIL *removes* PARHAM'S *body from the stage.*)

ARDELL. Thin and frail.

SGT. TOWER. Gen'l'men, can you hear me?

ARDELL. Yes, Sergeant.

SGT. TOWER. I saw this rifle one time get blown right outa this boy's hands and him start wailin' and carryin' on right there how he ain't ever goin' back on no line, he'll die for sure, he don't have that one rifle in all the world. You listenin' to me, gen'l'men. I'm gonna tell you now what you do when you lost and it black, black night. The North Star show you true North accurate all year round. You gonna see the big dipper and two stars on the end called the pointer and they where the water would come on outa that dipper if it had water in it, and straight out from there is this big damn star and once you know North you ain't lost no more! (*And toward the end of this* PAVLO *has appeared, rising up from the back of the set, walking slowly as in a dream, looking at* SGT. TOWER.)

PAVLO. YES, SERGEANT! (*And an explosion hits;* PAVLO, *yelling, goes down again.*)

ARDELL. What you sayin'? YES, SERGEANT. What you sayin'? (*Perhaps also having fallen with the explosion.*)

PAVLO. YES, SERGEANT! (*Struggling to rise, as distantly,* D., *drifting,* YEN *enters and moves soundlessly to a place to kneel.*)

ARDELL. Ask him what about Ardell? What about Ardell layin' on that trail, that grenade come rollin' out the bushes, he scoop it under him. How come, if he's so cool, if he's such a fox, he don't know nothin' to do with no grenade but lay down on it? You walkin', talkin' scar, what you think you made of?

PAVLO. I got my shit together.

ARDELL. HOW MANY TIMES YOU GONNA LET 'EM HIT YOU?

PAVLO. AS MANY TIMES AS THEY WANT.

ARDELL. That man up there a fool, Jim.

PAVLO. Shut up.

ARDELL. You ever seen any North Star in your life?

PAVLO. I seen a lot of people pointin'. (PAVLO *is on the move toward* YEN *now.*)

ARDELL. They a bunch a fools pointin' at the air. "Go this way, go that way."

PAVLO. I want her, man. I need her. (*In some way touching her.*)

ARDELL. Where you now? What you doin'?

PAVLO. I'm with her, man.

ARDELL. You . . . in . . . her . . .

PAVLO. . . . soon . . . (PAVLO *is taking her blouse off her.*)

ARDELL. Why you there . . .

PAVLO. I dunno . . . jus' wanna . . .

ARDELL. You jus' gonna ride . . .

PAVLO. I jus' wanna . . .

ARDELL. There was one boy walkin' . . .

PAVLO. I know, don't talk no shit. (*Seizing her, embracing her.*)

ARDELL. Walkin' . . . singin' . . . soft, some song to himself, thinkin' on mosquitoes and Coke and bug spray until these bushes in front of him burst and his fine young legs broke in half like sticks . . .

PAVLO. Leave me alone! (*Rising, trying to get off his own trousers.*)

ARDELL. At seven his tonsils been cut out; at twelve there's appendicitis. Now he's 20 and hurtin' and screamin' at his legs, and then the gun come back. It on a fixed traversing arc to tear his yellin' fuckin' head right off.

PAVLO. Good; it's Tanner; it's Weber. It's Smith and not Pavlo. Minneti, not Pavlo. Klaus and Weber. YOU. You motherfucker, lookin' at me. Not Pavlo, not ever.

ARDELL. You get a knife wound in the ribs.

PAVLO. It misses my heart. I'm clean.

ARDELL. You get shrapnel all up and down your back.

PAVLO. It's like a dozen fifteen bee stings, all up and down my back.

ARDELL. And there's people tellin' you you can go home if you wanna. It's your second wound. They're sayin' you can go home when you been hit twice and you don't even check. You wanna go back out, you're thinkin', get you one more gook, get you one more slope-head, make him know the reason why.

PAVLO. (*Whirling, scooping up a rifle from the floor.*) That's right. They're killin' everybody. They're fuckin' killin' everybody! (*The rifle is aimed at* ARDELL.)

ARDELL. Like it's gonna make a difference in the world, man, what you do; and somethin' made bad's gonna be all right with this one more you're gonna kill. Poor ole Ryan gets dinged round about Tay Ninh, so two weeks later in Phu Loi you blow away this goddamn farmer. . . .

FARMER. (*Waving in the distance.*) O.K., G.I., O.K.

ARDELL. And think you're addin' somethin' up. (*The* FARMER *wears Vietnamese work clothes, conical hat.*)

PAVLO. I blew him to fuckin' smithereens. He's there at twenty yards, wavin'.

FARMER. O.K., G.I., O.K. (*He sways in the distance, appearing to approach.*)

PAVLO. DUNG LYE. DUNG LYE. (*This is "Stop" in Vietnamese, yelled at the* FARMER.)

ARDELL. You don't know he's got satchel charges.

PAVLO. I do.

ARDELL. You don't know what he's got under his clothes.

PAVLO. I do. He's got dynamite all under his clothes. And I shoot him. (*Gunshot, as* PAVLO *fires. He will fire two more times: two more gunshots.*) I fuckin' shoot him. He's under me. I'm screamin' down at him. RYAN. RYAN. And he's lookin' up at me. His eyes squinted like he knows by my face what I'm sayin' matters to me so maybe it matters to him. And then, all of a sudden, see, he starts to holler and shout like he's crazy, and he's pointin' at his foot, so I shoot it. I shoot his foot and then he's screamin' and tossin' all over the ground, so I shoot into his head. I shot his head. And I get hit again. I'm standin' there over him and I get fuckin' hit again. They keep fuckin' hittin' me. (*EXPLOSION and* PAVLO *goes flying forward.*) I don't know where I'm at. In my head. . . . It's like I'm twelve . . . a kid again. Ardell, it's going to happen to meeeeeee? (*He is on the ground where he has been knocked, crawling.*)

ARDELL. What do you want me to do?

PAVLO. I don't want to get hit anymore.

ARDELL. What do you want me to do?

PAVLO. Tell me.

ARDELL. He was shot . . . layin' down under you, what did you see?

PAVLO. What?

ARDELL. He was squirmin' down under you in that ditch, what did you see?

PAVLO. I saw the grass . . . his head. . . .

ARDELL. Noooooooooo.

PAVLO. Help me. I saw the grass, his head. . . .

ARDELL. Don't you ever hear?

PAVLO. I want out, Ardell, I want out.

ARDELL. When you gonna hear me?

PAVLO. What are you tryin' to tell me? I saw blood . . . bits of brain. . . .

ARDELL. Noooooooooooo!

PAVLO. The grass, the grass. . . .

ARDELL. When you shot into his head, it was like you hit into your own head, fool!

PAVLO. NOOOOOOOO. WHAT?

ARDELL. IT WAS YOUR OWN.

PAVLO. NOOOOOOOOOO! (*As* ARDELL *has turned to* leave.) Don't leave me, you sonofabitch. (*And* ARDELL *has stopped, back turned, far* U.) JIVE MOTHER-FUCKIN' BULLSHIT! (*And* ARDELL *is gone.*) And I

stood . . . lookin' . . . down . . . at that black, black
Hudson River . . . there was stars in it. . . . I was
twelve . . . I remember. . . . (*He is turning toward*
YEN *who is kneeling, singing.*) I went out toward them
. . . diving . . . down. . . . (*He is moving toward*
YEN, *crawling.*) They'd said there was no current, but
I was twisted in all that water, fighting to get up . . .
all my air burning out, couldn't get no more. . . . (*He
is moving toward* YEN.) and I was going down, fighting to get down. I was all confused, you see, fighting
to get down, thinking it was up. I hit sand. I pounded. I
pounded the bottom. I thought the bottom was the top.
Black. No air. (*As the officer enters, striding swiftly.*)

OFFICER. YES! (*Carries a clipboard on which he writes
as* PAVLO *runs up to him.* YEN, *though she remains kneeling, stop singing.* PAVLO *salutes.*)

PAVLO. Sir! I've just been released from Ward 17,
gunshot wound in my side, and I've been ordered back
to my unit, Second of the 16th, 1st Division, and I don't
think I should have to go. This is the third time I been
hit. I been hit in the ribs and leg and back. . . . I
think there should be more trainin' in duckin' and
dodgin', sir. I been hit by a knife, shrapnel and bullets.

OFFICER. Could you get to the point?

PAVLO. That is the point. I want to know about this
regulation sayin' you can go home after your second
wounding?

OFFICER. Pardon, Hummel?

PAVLO. I been told there's this regulation you can go
home after your second wound. When you been hit twice,
you can go home.

OFFICER. Hummel, wouldn't you be home if you were
were eligible to be home?

PAVLO. I don't know, sir; but I wanted to stay the
first two times, so I don't know and I was told I had the
option the second time to go home or not, but I never

checked and if I passed it by, sir, I'd like to go back and pick it up.

OFFICER. You didn't pass it by; there's no such regulation.

PAVLO. It was a sergeant who told me.

OFFICER. These orders are valid.

PAVLO. Could you check, sir?

OFFICER. I'm an expert on regulations, Hummel. These orders are valid. You've earned the Purple Heart. Now, go on back and do your job. (*Raising his hand to salute, pivots, exits as* PAVLO *is about to salute.*)

ARDELL. NO! NO!

PAVLO. I do my job.

(SGT. WALL *enters the bar, calling to* YEN *who moves quickly to the bar area where she pets him and then moves to prepare a drink for him.*)

SGT. WALL. Come here, Pretty Piggy, we talk boucoup love; okay? Make plans go my home America.

YEN. Sow.

SGT. WALL. No lie.

SGT. TOWER. (*In a kind of brooding, mournful rage atop his tower as* PAVLO *stands before him, looking up, listening, watching.*) Gen'l'men, lemme tell you what you do, the enemy got you, he all around you. You the prisoner. You listenin', gen'l'men?

ARDELL. Yes, Sergeant. (*All despairing sarcasm.*)

SGT. TOWER. You got to watch out for the enemy. He gonna try to make you feel alone and you got no friends but him. He gonna make you mean and afraid; then he gonna be nice. We had a case with them North Koreans, this group a American P.O.W.s, one of 'em was wounded so he cried all night. His buddies couldn't sleep. So, one night his buddies picked him up, I'm tellin' you, they carried him out the door into that North Korean winter, they set him down in the snow, they lef' him there, went on back inside. They couldn't hear him screamin' the wind was so loud. They got their sleep. You got to watch out for the enemy.

(PAVLO *pivots, turning away from* SGT. TOWER *and into the bar, where* MAMASAN *greets him and* YEN *is with* SGT. WALL *who wears civilian clothes: flowered, short-sleeved shirt and trousers.*)

MAMASAN. Paaablooooo . . . how you-you. I give you beer, okay?

PAVLO. (*Unmoving, rigid.*) Mamasan, Chow Ba.

SGT. WALL. (*This above occurring as the* SERGEANT *finishes a big drink as if mid-sentence, pours more, sets the bottle down.*) ". . . so who," he says, "was the first motherfucker to sail 'round the world? Not Vasco Da Gama." I don't know what he's sayin'. "Who was the first motherfucker to measure the ocean?" (*He is loud and waving his arms.*) I don't know! He wasn't even asking. MAMASAN! MAMASAN! ONE BEER! ONE BEER, ONE SAIGON TEA! (*He reaches now to take* YEN'S *hand and tug her gently around to his side of the table, drawing her near to sit on his lap.*) Come here; sit down. No sow. Fini sow. Beaucoup love Co Yen. Beaucoup love. (*His hand on her breast, as she nibbles his ear.*)

YEN. I think you maybe papasan America. Have many babysan.

SGT. WALL. No . . . no.

YEN. I think you sow.

SGT. WALL. No lie, Yen. No wife America, no have babysan. Take you, okay?

PAVLO. Sarge! (*Slight pause as* SGT. WALL *looks up to* PAVLO.) Listen; I don't have too much time, I got to go pretty soon; how long you gonna be talkin' shit to that poor girl? I mean, see, she's the whore I usually hit on, I'm a little anxious, I'd like to interrupt you, you gonna be at her all fuckin' night. I'll bring her back in half an hour.

SGT. WALL. Sorry about that. Sorry—

PAVLO. I didn't ask you was you sorry.

SGT. WALL. This little girl's my girl.

PAVLO. She's a whore, man—

SGT. WALL. We got a deal, see, see; and when I'm here, she stays with me.

PAVLO. You got a deal, huh?

SGT. WALL. You guessed it, Pfc.

PAVLO. Well, maybe you shoulda checked with me— you shoulda conferred with me maybe before you figured that deal was sound.

SGT. WALL. You have been informed.

PAVLO. But you don't understand, Sarge, she's the only whore here who move me.

SGT. WALL. My baby.

PAVLO. You rear-echelon asshole!

SGT. WALL. (*Beginning to rise.*) What's that?

PAVLO. Where you think you are, the goddamn P.X.? This the garbage dump, man, and you don't tell me nothin' down here let alone who I can hit on, who I can't hit on, you see what I'm sayin' to you, Fuckface.

YEN. Paablo . . . no, no. . . .

PAVLO. You like this ole man.

YEN. Can be nice, Paablo . . . (*Moving to face* PAVLO *and explain.*)

PAVLO. Old man. Papasan. Can do fuck-fuck maybe one time one week. Talk, talk. Talk. No can do boom-boom. PAPASAN. NUMBA FUCKIN' TEN!

YEN. Shut up. Paablo, I do him. Fini him. Do you. O.K. (*Angry at his stupidity.*)

PAVLO. Shut up?

SGT. WALL. You heard her.

PAVLO. Shut up? (*His hand twisting in her hair.*) I don't know who you think this bitch is, Sarge, but I'm gonna fuck her whoever you think she is. I'm gonna take her in behind those curtains and I'm gonna fuck her right side up and then maybe I'm gonna turn her over, get her in her asshole, you understand me? You don't like it you best come in pull me off.

SGT. WALL. (*Switchblade popping open in his hand.*) I ain't gonna have to, PUNK.

(*And* PAVLO *kicks him squarely in the groin. The man yells, falls.*)

PAVLO. The fuck you ain't. Hey . . . were you ready for that? Were you ready for that, ole man? Called crawlin', you gettin' (*Dragging the man along the ground, shoving him.*) the hang of it, you ole man. Get up, get up. (*And the man moans as* PAVLO *lifts him.*) I want you gone, you mother, you understand. I don't wanna see you no more. You gonna disappear. You are gonna vanish. (*And he flings the old man,* SGT. WALL, *away.* SGT. WALL *staggers, falls, and* PAVLO *picks the knife off the floor, goes for a beer as* SGT. TOWER *begins to speak and* SGT. WALL, *grenade in hand, circles.*)

SGT. TOWER. This a grenade, gen'l'men. M26A2 fragmentation, 5.5 ounces, composition B, time fuse, 13 feet a coiled wire inside it like the inside a my fist a animal and I open it and that ANIMAL LEAP OUT TO KILL YOU. Do you know a hunk a paper flyin' fast enough cut you in half like a knife, and when this baby hit, fifteen meters in all directions, ONE THOUSAND HUNKS A WIRE GOIN' FAST ENOUGH! (*And* ARDELL *enters, joining* PAVLO, *who celebrates.*)

PAVLO. Did I do it to him, Ardell? The triple Hummel? Got to be big and bad. A little shuffle. Did I ever tell you? Thirteen months a my life ago.

YEN. Paaaabiloooo, boucoup love!

PAVLO. Thirteen months a my life ago. (*And* SGT. WALL, *pulling pin on the grenade, is there in the corner, beginning to move.*) What she did my ole lady, she called Joanna a slut and I threw kitty litter, screamin'—cat shit—"happy birthday!" She called that sweet church-goin' girl a whore. To be seen by her now, up tight with this odd-lookin' whore, feelin' good and tall, ready to bed down. Feelin'— (*And the grenade lands, having been thrown by* SGT. WALL, *moving in a semicircle and fleeing.* PAVLO *drops to his knees seizing the grenade, looking up in awe at* ARDELL. *The grenade in* PAVLO'S *hands in his lap.*) Oh Christ!

(*And the explosion is there, now loud, it is a storm going into darkness and changing lights. Silence.* BODY DETAIL *enters as* ARDELL, *looking at* PAVLO *lying there begins to speak. The* BODY DETAIL *will wrap* PAVLO *in a poncho, put him on a stretcher, carry him to* ARDELL.)

ARDELL. He don't die right off. Take him four days, 38 minutes. And he don't say nothin' to nobody in all that time. No words; he just kinda lay up and look and when he die, he bitin' on his lower lip, I don't know why. So they take him, they put him in a blue rubber bag, zip it up tight and haul him off to the morgue in the back of a quarter ton where he get stuck naked into the refrigerator 'long with the other boys killed that day and the beer and cheese and tuna and stuff the guys who work at the morgue keep in the refrigerator except when it inspection time. The bag get washed, hung out to dry on a line out back a the morgue. (*Slight pause.*) Then . . . lemme see, well, finally, he get shipped home and his mother cry a lot and his brother get so depressed he gotta go out and lay his chippie he so damn depressed about it all; and Joanna, she read his name in the paper, she let out this little gasp and say to her husband across the table, "Jesus, Jimmy, I used to go with that boy. Oh, damn that war, why can't we have peace? I think I'll call his mother." Ain't it some kinda world? (*And he is laughing.*) Soooooooo . . . that about it. That about all I got to say. Am I right, Pavlo? Did I tell you true? You got anything to say? Oh, man, I know you do, you say it out. (*Slight pause as* ARDELL *moves to uncover* PAVLO.)

Man, you don't say it out, I don't wanna know you. Be
cool as you wanna be, Pavlo! Beee cool; lemme hear you.
. . . You tell it to me: what you think of the cause?
What you think a gettin' your ass blown clean off a free-
dom's frontier? What you think a bein' R.A. regular
army lifer?

PAVLO. (*Softly, with nearly embarrassed laughter.*)
Sheeeeee . . . ittttt . . . Oh, lord . . . oh . . .

ARDELL. Ain't it what happened to you? Lemme hear
it.

PAVLO. . . . Shit!

ARDELL. And what you think a all the "folks back
home," sayin' you a victim . . . you a animal . . . you
a fool . . .

PAVLO. They shit!

ARDELL. Yeh, baby; now I know you. It all shit.

PAVLO. It all shit!

ARDELL. You my man again.

PAVLO. It shit.

ARDELL. Lemme hear it! My *main* man.

PAVLO. SHIT!

ARDELL. Main motherfuckin' man.

PAVLO. OH, SHIT!

ARDELL. GO!

PAVLO. SHIT!

ARDELL. GET IT! GET IT!

PAVLO. (*A howl into silence.*) SHHHHHHHHHIIII-
IIIIITTTTTTTTTTTTTTtttttttt!

(*And* FOUR MEN *enter carrying the aluminum box of a
coffin, while two other men go across the back of the
stage doing the drill, the marching and twirling rifles
that were done at the end of the first act. They go
now, however, in the opposite direction, and the coffin is placed beside* PAVLO.)

ARDELL. That right. How you feel? You feel all right?
You gotta get that stuff outta you, man. You body know

that and you body smart; you don't get that outta you, it back up on you, man, poison you.

(*The* FOUR MEN *are placing* PAVLO *in the coffin.*)

PAVLO. But . . . I . . . am dead!

(*The* MEN *turn and leave. There is no precision in anything they do. All is casual, daily work.*)

ARDELL. Got wings as big as streets; got large, large wings. (*Slight pause.*) You want me to talk shit to you? Man, sure, we siftin' things over. We in a bar, man, back home, we got good soft chairs, beer in our hands, Go-Go Girls all around; one of 'em got her eye on you, 'nother one thinkin' little bit on me. You believe what I'm sayin'. You *home*, Pavlo. (*Pause.*) Now . . . you c'mon and you be with me. . . . We gonna do a little singin'. You be with me. Saw some stockin's . . . on the street. . . . (*Silence.*)

PAVLO. Saw some . . . stockin's . . . on . . . the street. . . .

ARDELL. (*Slight pause.*) . . . wished I was . . . between those . . . feet . . .

PAVLO. Wished I was between those feet! (*Slight pause.*)

ARDELL and PAVLO. (*Together.*) Once a week, I get to town, they see me comin', they jus' lay down . . .

ARDELL. Sergeant, Sergeant, can't you see . . .

PAVLO. Sergeant, Sergeant, can't you see . . .

ARDELL. All this misery's killin' . . . me . . .

PAVLO. All this misery's killin'—

ARDELL. (*Lets the coffin close; it thus, cutting* PAVLO *off.*)

    Ain't no matter what you do . . .
    Jody done it . . . all to you . . .
       (*Slight pause:* ARDELL *is backing away.*)

Lift your heads and lift 'em high . . .
Pavlo Hummel . . . passin' by . . .
    (ARDELL *turns, begins to walk away.*)

(As ARDELL *disappears* U., *the coffin stands in REAL
LIGHT.)*

PROP LIST

12 rifles (M-16's or M-14's)
3 army beds, sheets, blankets, etc.
4 bottles of Vietnamese beer
3 army footlockers
1 paper bag, bottle of aspirin and glue
1 gas mask
1 shovel
2 utility belts, canteens
3 army towels
2 comic books
1 ammunitions box (used as seat)
1 army 15 gallon drum (used as seat)
American money—bills
1 deck playing cards
1 wallet
2 stretchers, ponchos
1 set civilian clothes on hanger
1 army blanket
Bayonets and bullet clips for rifles
1 pair dice
1 harmonica
1 pair sunglasses
1 notice (trainees passed-failed)
1 broom
1 pool table, 2 cues, 2 chalks and 1 cue ball
1 dress uniform in garment bag (HUMMEL)
1 pair boots (HUMMEL)
2 grenades
1 can of Coke
2 Gerry Cans (used as seat)
2 Gerry cans (used as seat)
1 medic bag
1 utility belt, .45 automatic pistol
1 carrying sling
1 telephone
1 duffel bag
1 day bag
1 bedspread

Wallet, keys, watch, money (MICKEY)
1 folder, army forms
1 clipboard, army forms and pen
3 cans American beer (Budweiser)
1 bottle of whiskey
1 trik knife
1 switchblade
1 cloth gag
1 utility belt, concealed rubber bulb and blood
1 M-1 rifle
1 coffin
1 false bottom bed, movable (BRISBEY)
1 chart holder, x-rays
1 tray, needle, cotton, alcohol and serum
1 bottle of liquor and two glasses
Vietnamese money—bills
1 rubber sheet

COSTUME LIST

ACT ONE

PAVLO:
Regulation U.S. Army basic training fatigues
White T shirts and boxer shorts
Dog tags
Removable P.f.c. stripes
Tailored dress greens
2 pairs of army boots

ARDELL:
Regulation U.S. Army dress khaki (shirt and pants)
Boots
Dark green overseas cap
Dog tags
Black aiguilettes

SERGEANT TOWER:
Regulation U.S. Army drill sgt. uniform
Boots
Ascot

CORPORAL:
Regulation camouflage fatigues
Boots
Dog tags

CAPTAIN:
Regulation basic training fatigues
Ascot
Boots

YEN:
Silk Oriental shirts and pants
Thong sandals

KRESS:

PARKER:

PIERCE:

HINKLE: U.S. Army Basic training fatigues

RYAN:

VARIOUS SOLDIERS:

ACT TWO

PAVLO:
  Regulation U.S. Army jungle fatigues
  Jungle boots
  O.D. T shirt and boxer shorts

MICKEY:
  Modern business suit
  Shirt
  Tie
  Shoes

MRS. HUMMEL:
  Nightgown
  House coat
  Slippers

SERGEANT JONES:
  Contemporary clothes (walking suit)
  Civilian shoes

MAMASAN:
  Oriental peasant clothes
  Thong sandals

BRISBEY:
  Hospital pajamas

SERGEANT WALL:
  Jungle fatigues
  Jungle boots
  Civilian clothes
  Civilian shoes

GIRL VIETCONG: ⎫
                ⎬ Oriental peasant clothes
BOY VIETCONG: ⎭
Various soldiers:
  In Regulation jungle fatigues

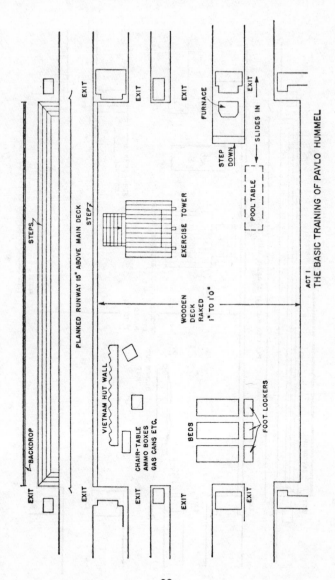

ACT I
THE BASIC TRAINING OF PAVLO HUMMEL

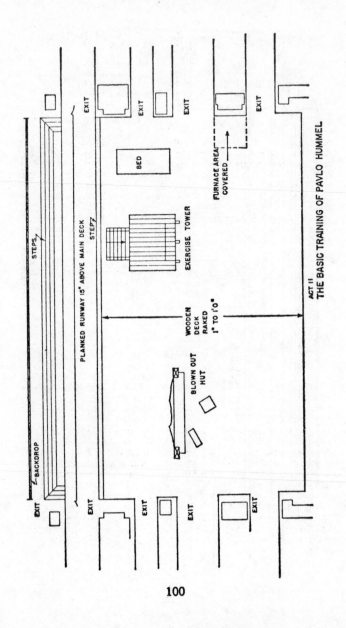

STEPS

BACKDROP

EXIT

PLANKED RUNWAY 15" ABOVE MAIN DECK

STEPS

EXIT

EXIT

EXIT

BED

EXERCISE TOWER

FURNACE AREA
COVERED

EXIT

WOODEN
DECK
RAKED
1" TO 1'0"

BLOWN OUT
HUT

EXIT

EXIT

EXIT

EXIT

EXIT

ACT II
THE BASIC TRAINING OF PAVLO HUMMEL

GOLDEN FLEECING

By LORENZO SEMPLE, JR.

FARCE

11 men, 2 women—Interior

When the Navy pays a courtesy call in Venice, a lieutenant, together with an ensign and a civilian scientist, takes up residence in a plush hotel in order to execute a fantastic scheme: with the aid of a spotter in a local roulette palace they are going to relay numbers from one particular wheel to the secret computer aboard a cruiser, and by a scientific calculation of odds break the bank of Venice. But a couple of lovely girls prove too distracting for our schemers. The lieutenant falls head-over-heels for the one who turns out to be the admiral's daughter; and when the admiral himself appears, all their plans are compromised.

The scientist runs into his old fiancee, now engaged to a pompous windbag. Deftly the author tightens the noose on the schemers, as they go from the frying pan into the fire. In a blaze of signal lights and counter-espionage speed, and with the mechanical-brain computer going full blast aboard ship, the curtain comes down on a peak of hilarity and innocent resolution.

(Royalty, $50-$25.)

The Private Ear ... The Public Eye

By PETER SHAFFER

The first, THE PRIVATE EAR, (2m., 1f.) is a rueful romance in which a boy makes a date with a girl he met at a concert, and has his worldly friend coach him for the occasion. Not only is the coaching all wrong for the occasion, but the girl turns out to be a very rude disappointment.

In THE PUBLIC EYE (2m., 1f.) we meet a snappy private detective who dresses like an unmistakable neon sign and is constantly eating yogurt and grapefruit. He has been hired to tail an accountant's wife, but has succeeded in giving himself away every time. "The twin comedies are delightful any way you want to look at them. They are deftly contrived, cheerfully entertaining."—*N.Y. Herald Tribune.* "They are silky-smooth, literate, witty and irresistibly human."—*Daily News.* "At the conclusion of each you know that you have been a guest at two lucid moments of truth."—*N.Y. World-Telegram & Sun.*

(Royalty, $25-$15 each, or $30-$25 together.)

DON'T DRINK THE WATER

By WOODY ALLEN

FARCE

12 men, 4 women—Interior

A CASCADE OF COMEDY FROM ONE OF OUR FUNNIEST CO-MEDIANS, and a solid hit on Broadway, this affair takes place inside an American embassy behind the Iron Curtain. An American tourist, caterer by trade, and his family of wife and daughter rush into the embassy two steps ahead of the police, who suspect them of spying and picture-taking. But it's not much of a refuge, for the ambassador is absent and his son, now in charge, has been expelled from a dozen countries and the whole continent of Africa. Nevertheless, they carefully and frantically plot their escape, and the ambassador's son and the caterer's daughter even have time to fall in love. "Because Mr. Allen is a working comedian himself, a number of the lines are perfectly agreeable . . . and there's quite a delectable bit of business laid out by the author and manically elaborated by the actor. . . . The gag is pleasantly outrageous and impeccably performed."—*N. Y. Times.* "Moved the audience to great laughter. . . . Allen's imagination is daffy, his sense of the ridiculous is keen and gags snap, crackle and pop."—*N. Y. Daily News.* "It's filled with funny lines. . . . A master of bright and hilarious dialogue."—*N. Y. Post.*

(Slightly restricted. Royalty, $50-$25, where available.)

THE ODD COUPLE

By NEIL SIMON

COMEDY

6 men, 2 women—Interior

NEIL SIMON'S THIRD SUCCESS in a row begins with a group of the boys assembled for cards in the apartment of a divorced fellow, and if the mess of the place is any indication, it's no wonder that his wife left him. Late to arrive is another fellow who, they learn, has just been separated from his wife. Since he is very meticulous and tense, they fear he might commit suicide, and so go about locking all the windows. When he arrives, he is scarcely allowed to go to the bathroom alone. As life would have it, the slob bachelor and the meticulous fellow decide to bunk together—with hilarious results. The patterns of their own disastrous marriages begin to reappear in this arrangement; and so this too must end. "The richest comedy Simon has written and purest gold for any theatregoer. . . . This glorious play."—*N. Y. World-Telegram & Sun.* "His skill is not only great but constantly growing. . . . There is scarcely a moment that is not hilarious."—*N. Y. Times.*

(Royalty, $50-$35.)

NEVER TOO LATE

by SUMNER ARTHUR LONG

FARCE

6 men, 3 women—Interior

Paul Ford split the seams all up and down Broadway with this portrait of a married man in his fifties who suddenly learns that he is to become a father again. His last child was a girl, born 24 years ago, and considering the boob she ended up marrying, he finds the prospect of another such affair unthinkable. Well, he has some point there. His daughter and son-in-law are still living with him, and he has a firsthand picture of how they turned out, with daughter never getting up to eat breakfast before lunch, and with the son-in-law curiously addicted to solitaire—a habit he avers he could kick if he once put his mind to it. The announcement of the baby, however, is not all that is to startle him. For at long last his meek little wife puts her foot down and issues some terms of her own. There's going to be a nursery, and a new bath, and she is going to have her checking account. Such a dour capitulation you will never see again in your life. "Something we have not had in the theatre in a long, long time is a good old-fashioned domestic farce . . . I realized I'd been missing something lately—plain and simple laughter."—*N.Y. Daily News.*

(Royalty, $50-$25.)

A THURBER CARNIVAL

By JAMES THURBER

REVUE

5 men, 4 women—Periaktoe, and Travellers

Winner of special Tony Award, this is a revue for those with no musical talent created by America's leading humorist, James Thurber, and first performed in New York by Tom Ewell, Peggy Cass, Paul Ford, and Alice Ghostley. The famous Don Elliott Quartet played some fine modern compositions of their own between scenes, but nothing really got in the way of these sketches of tumbling American life. Here you will find the famous: "The Night the Bed Fell;" the fable of the unicorn in the garden (Don't count your boobies until they're hatched," says the husband as his wife is carted away in the jiffy wagon); and "Gentlemen Shoppers," which is fine shopping spree for two men as long as the martinis flow. "Of bellylaughs there is an abundance . . . Small, cozy, and completely captivating revue . . . 'The Thurber Carnival' is sheer delight."—*N.Y. Herald Tribune.* "A clean, lovable crackling of sharp fun."—*N.Y. World-Telegram & Sun.* "A joyous, magnificently lunatic festival . . . Remember this address and hie you thence, for oh, that way madness lies."—*N.Y. News.*

(Royalty, $50-$25.)

A COMMUNITY OF TWO

JEROME CHODOROV

(All Groups) Comedy

4 Men, 3 Women, Interior

Winner of a Tony Award for "Wonderful Town." Co-author of "My Sister Eileen," "Junior Miss," "Anniversary Waltz." This is a charming off-beat comedy about Alix Carpenter, a fortyish divorcee of one month who has been locked out of her own apartment and is rescued by her thrice-divorced neighbor across the hall, Michael Jardeen. During the course of the two hours in which it takes to play out the events of the evening, we meet Alix's ex-husband, a stuffed shirt from Wall Street, her son, who has run away from prep school with his girl, heading for New Mexico and a commune. Michael's current girl friend, Olga, a lady anthropologist just back from Lapland, and Mr. Greenberg, a philosopher-locksmith. All take part in the hilarious doings during a blizzard that rages outside the building and effects everybody's lives. But most of all, and especially, we get to know the eccentric Michael Jardeen, and the confused and charming Alix Carpenter, who discover that love might easily happen, even on a landing, in the course of a couple of hours of highstress living.

"Thoroughly delightful comedy."—*St. Louis-Post Dispatch.* "A joy."—*Cleveland Plain Dealer.* "Skillful fun by Jerome Chodorov."—*Toronto Globe Star.*

ROYALTY, $50-$35

ROMAN CONQUEST

JOHN PATRICK

(All Groups) Comedy

One set—3 Women, 6 Men

The romantic love story of two American girls living in the romantic city of Rome in a romantic garret at the foot of the famous Spanish steps. One of the world's richest young women takes her less fortunate girl friend to Italy to hide unknown and escape notoriety while she attempts to discover if she has any talent as an artist—free of position and prestige. Their misadventures with language and people supply a delightful evening of pure entertainment. Remember the movies "Three Coins in the Fountain" and "Love Is A Many Splendored Thing"? This new comedy is in the same vein by the same Pulitzer Prize winning playwright.

ROYALTY, $50-$35